WAKING UP

LIVING OPEN

HANNAH WALTON

hailee,
Believe in
your story.

♡ Hannah

Cover Art by Taylor Perkey

Scripture quotations are taken from the *Holy Bible,* New Living Translation, copyright ©1996, 2004, 2007, 2013, 2015 by Tyndale House Foundation. Used by permission of Tyndale House Publishers, Inc., Carol Stream, Illinois 60188. All rights reserved.

Contents

Introduction

I remember that night, not as clearly as I once did, but the memory remains nonetheless. I found myself crying a mix of hopeless desperation and decided defeat. I was giving up. I knew what I hoped for, what I wanted, but I also knew the reality of it all – the one I had steadily built up for myself over time. I was not my own worst enemy; I was the best. I had become an expert on the grounds of self-destruction. Day after day and night after night, I watched with careless eye, as the flickering light of my strength grew increasingly dim. I had a front row seat to my own demise and I was almost apathetic in realizing that all I had been holding onto was collapsing. I was only fifteen, and yet I was convinced that my whole world was crashing down. And I was ready to go down with it. I had made up my mind and this was it. That night I made a choice. The next morning, I woke up alive.

I have seen great pain, but I have known great Joy.

I started writing this book when I was seventeen years old. Early in my journey with Jesus, I realized the significance of the story – the one He was writing with my life. I became aware that my struggles were preparation and I developed a fierce determination to press through pain, discouragement, and fear. I often fell (and still fall) short, but I'm grateful for the constant reminder that it is not by might or power but by *His* Spirit (Zechariah 4:6, emphasis mine).

My vision came into clearer focus as I started seeing the testimony on the other side of my struggles and hardships, even at a young age. Bad things happen. Yes, God sometimes allows them to, but He does not inflict pain on His own. A mentor once taught me that everything in life is "Father-filtered," used for our good and for His glory, to strengthen our endurance, character, faith, and hope (Romans 5:3-4). We live in a fallen world, so unfortunately pain and tough times are a part of the package deal.

"But God…" The interjecting reassurance

found throughout Scripture to remind us that in all circumstances, there is hope for a divine intervening. For every bit of bad, there is a Redeemer. He is in the business of turning things around. Joseph said it well when he said, "You intended to harm me, but God intended it all for good."[1]

I remember going to youth events with my church as a teenager and hearing people's stories in the services. I remember how impactful and inspiring it was to hear about their overcoming and all that they had discovered in the process. It gave me hope and encouragement for my own story. While I was a student at Christ for the Nations Institute in Dallas, Texas, I heard a lecture by Dutch Sheets in which he explained the meaning of the word "testimony." Though commonly thought of in terms of saying something over again, it actually means, "to do again." So when we talk about what God has done in our lives, it releases the same power that changed us to move, encourage, and inspire yet again. That is how we overcome by the blood of the Lamb *and* the word of our testimony.

So here is mine. In telling you my story, my hope is that you will be able to find pieces that relate to your own, that you will understand and feel understood. I hope it releases that same power of hope, healing, freedom and life to you as you read, and I pray it will inspire you to share your story as well.

Dear God,

Hey… I'm not exactly sure what you're doing in my life. I trust you, it just hurts. All I feel right now is pain. What am I here for? I feel stupid, ugly, and worthless. I ruin all the good. I don't understand why any of this is happening. How could you leave me in this condition? You took away everything. I love you and I want to serve you with all my life, I do, but right now I'm empty. I can't feel you here with me. I feel alone, like everyone is turning on me. I can't trust anyone here. Nobody understands me. I don't know anyone I can talk to about the way I'm hurting. Right now you must be disappointed in me too. Please forgive me. I was just so scared, so hurt. Please don't leave me. I'm going to try to trust you with my heart, with everything. Just give me reminders that you're in control, that you have a plan, and that everything will be okay. I'm broken, but you are still my joy. Sustain me.

1
The Beginning: Anything Can Happen

It's funny how we often don't appreciate things until we are looking back at them. I grew up in Burleson, Texas. I somehow ended up being born to the most incredible parents I could have ever asked for, and soon after me came my brother, David. Life was good. We were provided for, nurtured, and accepted. Our home was safe and kind, and all was well in my little world. I remember our weekend day trips, playing in the backyard with my dad, and exploring the ups and downs of childhood with David. Although we had our typical sibling arguments from time to time, we loved each other and now consider each other "homies."

We were blessed to have a mom who was able to stay at home with us. I got to know her well and never doubted whether she cared about us. No mother is perfect, but if you knew mine, then you'd know she loves people well. I got to see her reaching out to broken and hurting people all the time. She invited everyone she knew to be a part of the hope she had found in Jesus. She and my dad make a great team. My dad has always been a hard worker. He pushed us to achieve excellence when we were kids, but assured us that it was because he knew what we were capable of. I will always be grateful for that, even though it drove me crazy at the time. He would do anything for anyone, and in my eyes, he is the most humble and content man I have ever known. But more than any of that, the greatest thing my parents ever were for me was *there*. I knew I could always count on them if I needed anything. No words could ever fully express how thankful I am for who they are and all they have done for me.

I say none of this to brag; only for the sake of honesty, because I didn't always see my parents like this. Trust me when I say we had our fair share of disagreements, yelling, and frustration. It was a long time before I realized what I had in front of me. I didn't always appreciate my parents. In fact, there were days I thought they would never understand me or even let me breathe. But Dr. Phil was so right when he said, "Hindsight's 20/20."

For some time, I was convinced that my parents were punishing me unfairly with their strict discipline and what I considered "over-protection" at times. I didn't see that the boundaries they put in place really were for my benefit and protection, but now I can recognize that it was love motivating their decisions all along.

Years later, I can clearly see the same heart in our Father God. If I had understood that His instructions – though difficult, uncomfortable, and painful at times – are only to keep us from harm, I would have responded much more quickly in obedience on so many occasions.

I started going to church the Sunday after I was born and I went to the same private Christian school from first grade until the time I graduated. I had Bible class every day at school and chapel on Wednesdays, I was at some sort of church service at least twice a week, and I knew a whole lot *about* God, but I never really knew God. I had a general idea of who He is and what He's about. I knew the stories. I knew that He is good and loves me and is worthy of praise, but I never really gave Him much of my attention. I had no clue that so much more was available.

When I was in sixth grade, it was time for me to move up into the youth group at the church we attended at the time, and I was so excited to finally be a part of it. I had looked up to them for as long as I could remember and couldn't wait to be right there with them. When the time came, however, it did not go as I had hoped or expected. I felt like I didn't fit in. Most of the kids in the youth group went to school together, and I felt like an outsider because I went to private school. I wasn't as pretty as a lot of the other girls were, and some of the boys made jokes about that. I talked myself into believing I didn't belong, that I was different. A list of reasons why I was "less than" and not enough began to accumulate in my mind.

The same thing started happening at school, and comments rolled in online as well. People were saying things about me and the way that I looked that I had never considered before, and I became increasingly self-aware. For the first time in my life my eyes were opened to the concept of others perceiving me much differently than the "me" I thought I was. I was hurt and confused and sad and lonely because around the same time, many of my friendships were falling apart. It was the time in life when people were changing, making new friends, and dealing with their own problems. People were moving on and I felt left behind. I felt alone. Insecure. Afraid. Misunderstood. I bought into the lies that had been only a whisper at first, and I unknowingly crafted a reality for myself completely based on them. The pain and rejection caused me to shut down and the walls to come up – walls constructed by the whirlwind of emotions that exploded inside of me. (The normal adolescent hormones did not help.) Brick by brick, I slowly built up a world that I didn't realize was unstable until much later.

Fear grew and grew, as it always does in accordance with its expanding nature. I was afraid of being alone, of being rejected, of never truly being loved. I developed an extreme case of anxiety, and I knew from experience that it could attack at any moment if I were to allow the army of "what ifs" to get out of hand. My mom would sit on the side of my bed when I couldn't sleep and read me Psalm 91, a chapter she had told me helped her overcome fear when she was my age. I learned to turn to Jesus in the midst of pain. That turned out to be one valuable lesson, and I had no idea how much I would need to cling to it later on.

As weeks turned into months, the whispers that were once a gentle tug turned into a loud and violent pull. The words they had said about me never left me alone, and it didn't take long for the lies to fog my mind and divert my vision. I thought perhaps I had been wrong about myself all along. Maybe I *was* ugly. Maybe I *was* fat. Maybe, just maybe, I had seen myself incorrectly from the start. What happened?

Sadness grew and took root deep in my heart because fear told me it was safe there and that no one would understand anyway. I spent most of my time thinking about what other people thought about me, so much so that I neglected taking care of myself. I pushed myself aside and focused on how I could be "acceptable." I set impossible standards for myself and started striving for that unattainable perfection that so many of us chase after and never catch. It was like running on a treadmill trying to reach something in front of me that somehow kept moving farther and farther away. It didn't take me long to figure out that perfectionism only exhausts, but even that knowledge never slowed me down. Why do we do this to ourselves?

In the meantime, insecurity grew and sadness caused more fear, warning me not to let anyone else in, running from the possibility of more pain at all cost. Loneliness grew because I ran. And ran. And ran.

I was consumed. It began with insecurity, turned into fear and sadness, and eventually led to actions I thought were no big deal. I started giving away my food at school. I was scared to risk gaining weight and I wanted to be alone anyway, so I resorted to spending lunch breaks hiding in the bathroom or sitting by myself in the bleachers, thinking or writing, usually both. I was always writing. At the time, I thought no one valued my opinion, so I didn't share it. Most of the time I didn't stand up for myself or speak my mind. What difference would it make? I talked myself out of it any time I had the chance, figuring it wouldn't be worth it to make people like me even less.

Instead, I used a pen. I wrote my thoughts. I wrote my prayers, hoping that at some point they would make it all the way up to the ears of the God whom I had learned cared about my pain and somehow loved me, the mess I was.

After a while, I was no longer just striving; I was starving. I ran until all I had was myself and a bundle of lies I was tangled up in, feeling paralyzed and suffocated, like the life in me was slowly draining out so the lies could stay fed. It was a self-destructing cycle that had me fooled, and I didn't understand that the lies were growing because I had let them in. I didn't see that they were things I had decided to believe, and as a result, accepted them as my version of the truth. I didn't realize then that I had a choice. Most days I felt like a marionette puppet and I forgot I had a heartbeat of my own. Living with those lies and the others they invited along was a compromise that cost me a whole lot more than I had anticipated.

I developed an eating disorder at twelve years old. It started subtly, but snuck up on me quickly and progressed far past what I had planned. It started as simply giving away my lunch, but over the next six and a half years the restricting got more restrictive and what I saw in the mirror became less and less satisfactory.

It was my reality, but I often thought about how it didn't feel real. I wasn't really *that* bad. It wasn't *that* serious. I would keep strict records of my weight and intake. I would take pills and starve myself and go to the bathroom to throw up after I had eaten so much that it hurt, and at the time, it didn't seem like that big of a deal. I saw the shows and heard about the girls who "had it worse." But the truth is, we've been deceived. There are no degrees when it comes to hopelessness. You either have hope or you don't, no matter what your circumstances look like. And I did not.

It's like lies: they don't have to be complete opposites of the truth. Actually, the enemy will often trick us with a lie so close to the truth that it seems believable. But we have to be careful, because wandering even just one inch off the path can end up leading you to an entirely different destination. Even if it's only a small lie, it is not truth; even if it's only a small bit of hopelessness, it is not hope.

The hopeless reality I had built, or allowed to be built, tricked me into thinking I would survive. You see, hopelessness shows itself in a variety of ways. Even on the days when I was pulling through, and even when I did turn to Jesus desperate for comfort and real truth, my state of hopelessness robbed me of life. Although Jesus came to give me a full and abundant life, the enemy (the very father of lies) was killing, stealing, and destroying, because hopelessness remained, hovering over me like a thick cloud I inhaled with each breath (see John 10:10). It's like a scent you become accustomed to once you've settled into a place. Hopelessness disguised itself as an attitude of "Oh well" on the hard days, the "This is how it will always be" in the shame of my shortcomings, and the "I'm going to regret this" as I gave into temptation just one more time, thinking, *hoping*, it would be the last. Maybe next time I'd be strong enough to resist, but hopelessness held me in a faulty perspective that blurred my vision of the exit.

Hopelessness makes overcoming seem much further away than it really is. That's how lies work: they are a tool the enemy uses to distance us from our loving God. So how do we refocus? Truth. Truth sets you free (see John 8:32). This truth is the Word of God, the very Son held in the flesh of our humanity. The man Jesus, the absolute substance of hope (Colossians 1:27). When we come to know Him – *really* know Him – we are beautifully set free. Of course, there will be days of struggle, but the Word of God must be our filter for all that we believe. His truth is the perfect standard against which we must measure all things. The truth is that He really *is* who He says He is and He really *will* do what He says He'll do. This is the renewing of our minds, retraining our thought processes to keep our reality in tune with His, which is a life fashioned by a hope that is consistently woven throughout mountains and valleys.

As Hebrews 11 teaches us, faith is confident hoping. The more truth you get rooted into your heart, the more confident you will become. The more confident you become, the more sturdy your hope will be, and as a result, faith grows. And with faith, anything is possible.

Although the process of a reality being unwound can be painful in the exposure, the more you get to know Jesus, the more light will break through your darkness. With each bit of truth laid sturdy in your foundation, you will become stronger. Believe me in this, you will overcome.

2
Something Cold & Something New
(and the warmth that brought meaning to it all)

For a long time, I wondered what it would be like to have another sibling. I love David and I wouldn't trade him for anything, but I always thought it would be cool to have an older brother. I could hang out with him and his older friends, go to his sporting events, and he could drive me places. Or maybe I'd like a sister that I could talk to about girl stuff and go shopping with. She would be someone I could look up to and learn from. Sometimes I even thought about what it would be like to have a younger brother or sister that I could play with and read stories to. I thought that would be fun. Be careful what you wish for, right?

It was my seventh grade year and our family was preparing for a big change. After a long and stressful process of paperwork, organizing, and waiting, we were ready. We had decided to adopt. I was so excited to meet my new little sister! My mom and I had tossed around the idea of adoption quite a bit over the past couple of years, and she was all for it. We had several family friends who had adopted from all over the world, and with my parents' welcoming compassion and love for others, I thought it seemed a promising possibility for our family. However, my dad was not so convinced. He had reasonable concerns: the finances, the adjustments and sacrifices that would have to be made, the overall commitment. And he was right; it would not be a "quick and easy" process.

After a while, we got David on board. Now we just had to get Dad. Actually, I laugh now remembering how David and I would conveniently leave little scraps of paper laying around Dad's counter with Bible verses about loving the orphans written on them. At times, it was frustrating and I didn't understand why my dad resisted so much, but what I didn't know was that God was moving. He already had a plan, and was working out His perfect timing for it.

I have come to love this about our God: how we can try and try and try to change someone's mind about what we believe to be His will, but until they hear His voice for themselves, nothing will happen.

Oh, how we wear ourselves out trying to do these things through our own strength. But our God has a way of speaking right to our hearts. He knows each one of us entirely and completely, down to every minute detail. (If you don't believe me, read Luke 12:6-7. In fact, read it just because.) He knows where we're at and He knows how and when to speak to us in ways we will understand. He is a personal God. He is a Father. If it were up to us to make the difference, so many things would be done out of obligation. Change would be forced. If it were forced or pressured, it wouldn't be genuine, and for this reason it would not be sustained, as anything insincere tends to fade.

Our efforts end up hollow when they are rushed, forced, or backed by wrong motives. Max Lucado wrote, "God's efforts are strongest when our efforts are useless."[1] I don't think this means that God has more power when we move out of the way or surrender; rather, I believe that our weakness serves to magnify His infinite and immeasurable strength.[2] I don't believe God views our intentions and efforts as stupid or useless, and I don't think our weaknesses exasperate Him. I honestly do not believe that our God is up there, arms crossed, tapping His foot, waiting for us to get our act together. If that were the case, the love, mercy, and grace that Jesus embodies would cause Him to contradict Himself.

When it's God, real change happens. Mountains move, eyes are opened, and lives are transformed. God knows how to get His will accomplished. He gives us grace to get exactly where we need to be, do exactly what He leads us to do, and all right on time in accordance with His perfect plan. That's exactly what happened with our family. My parents both prayed and little by little, clarity came. At first, my dad agreed to adopt domestically; an American child would have a much easier transition than an international child. That was the plan for a while, until we went to an informational meeting about all the countries our adoption agency placed children from. We listened as they told us about each one, and when we left we all knew: the other Walton was in Ethiopia.

We couldn't believe it. Not only were we adopting internationally now; we were adopting an African child. We braced ourselves for the change as much as we could, but we knew that in an area that was predominantly white at the time, it was going to be a big change. We didn't mind the difference a bit, but we wondered what people would think and how our new sister or brother would feel. We tried not to worry and instead just continued to trust that God knew best. Months passed as we prepared for the new Walton. We had no idea what he or she would be like, but we were excited knowing God already had someone just for us.

The day finally came and the four of us gathered around the computer at Dad's office. The agency called and told us they had found someone they thought would fit into our family. We watched as Dad opened up the email and our eyes raced to the attachment. It was a picture of a little Ethiopian girl. She was four years old and so beautiful. Tears in our eyes, we looked at each other and knew she was the one. We said yes and moved forward with the adoption.

A couple months later, my parents boarded a plane while I was getting out of school for spring break. They were gone the whole week finalizing legal things and picking up our new sister, Kuri. I will never forget how cute she looked coming through those doors at the airport. She was so small, but she pushed the entire cart of luggage. This ambition and confidence has stuck with her. I hope it always will.

We brought Kuri home and began our new life as a family of five. As she stepped into a brand new world, it was beautiful and exciting to see the wonder in her eyes as she marveled at things I had grown used to and taken for granted. I remember that first Easter and how many times we must have hidden those eggs in our living room, cracking up at her shrieks when she discovered them all over again.

Some of the transitions were fun, like taking her to church and watching her learn English so quickly that no one would have believed she knew none just a few months before. But some transitions were hard. It was months before she would wear her seatbelt without screaming or fall asleep in her own bed. She had to learn her new name, meet her new family, obey the new rules. I'm sure it was a shock to her. I know it was a whole lot more than I had ever expected.

At first, I was so happy to have her home. I loved spending time with her and watching her grow, and I knew that us adopting her would change her life forever. It was such a beautiful concept, but I didn't consider at the time how different *my* life would be. I was no longer the only daughter. Mom couldn't say I was her favorite girl anymore. People had a new little girl to pamper and spoil with cute things, and I suddenly felt less important. Everyone was always checking on Kuri's progress and asking how she was doing, and although I understood, at times I felt forgotten.

I felt so selfish feeling that way. I was supposed to be excited and love Kuri and be a good big sister, setting an example for her to follow. We didn't get along. With the nine-year age gap and cultural differences, we did not see eye-to-eye. I didn't understand why it was so hard. I was so frustrated, but I knew my parents were dealing with their own stress from the adjustments and I didn't want anyone to think I was hateful toward Kuri or treating her badly, so I kept it to myself and let it boil up inside.

I was still trying to be "acceptable." I wanted so desperately to have it all together, but I was falling apart inside. I had a collection of emotions that I kept stuffed deep down where no one could see. I wore a mask at school and focused all my energy on being a good student. I knew Dad would be proud if I made straight A's and had all my assignments done on time. I wanted Mom to see that I was mature enough to take care of all my responsibilities and mind my own business.

I became absorbed with people pleasing. I resisted the thought of being considered selfish so much that I continued to lower myself on my priority list until I was hardly on it, thinking that if I just gave people what they wanted, I would be accepted and feel satisfied. I gave and gave and gave until I had nothing left to give. At the time I thought I was loving people really well, but looking back now I can see that it was just a frail effort to be loved in return – or at all.

Now, the crazy thing is, I *was* loved. I could never trace back to a time my parents didn't love me. I had friends who loved me and my teachers always made themselves available to me and cared about how I was doing. The disconnect was caused by the lies I was believing. The reason I didn't feel loved was because I had followed lies so far in one direction that I could barely decipher the truth. The voice we listen to is the loudest, so the more acquainted we become with the devil's whispers, the more we second-guess the Father's. The further we get from the truth, the harder it is to distinguish what's real and what isn't. I was convinced that if people really loved me, I would be happy and I wouldn't have these problems; if I were loved, I would have lots of attention and be more confident. But that's just not true.

It sounds so ridiculous now; however, that is honestly how I felt back then. But that isn't love. It's not even close. God is love (1 John 4:8) and satan will do whatever he can to try to separate us from this truth. That's why he has worked so hard to pervert and twist love in our world today. But love is so much more than our beliefs and society have made it out to be.[3] God's love is honest. It is patient, kind, and understanding. It keeps no record of wrongs and it doesn't give up.

I was loved. There is one time in particular where I remember a light trickling in through my darkness, a glimmer of hope that shook my perspective of what love was. Truth started to break in. Shortly after we adopted Kuri and right before my eighth grade year, we felt led to move to the church where David and I went to school.

As a result of the pain and rejection I had felt before, I isolated myself. I wanted nothing to do with the Church if it meant feeling that way again. The thought of starting over somewhere new did not appeal to me in the slightest because I knew there was the risk of not being accepted again. I had grown bitter and continued to linger in the grip of fear. Nevertheless, my parents dragged me along every Sunday and Wednesday and I stubbornly sat through services, disengaged and unwilling to give those people a chance.

Fortunately, many of the church people were also the school people, so there weren't as many strangers there. There were several other people from my class in the youth group. That helped some, but I was still holding onto the past and skeptically judging every bit of my present against it. Every now and then I would find myself intently listening to the message and then prayerfully contemplating my "whys" when I got home to the safety of my solitude again.

I remember wondering why things were the way they were. If Christians are supposed to be like Jesus, why are they so mean? Why do they say one thing and then do another? How could a Message that provides such hope and power be entrusted to such unreliable messengers?

It was years before I understood that it is purely because of His grace that God invites us into His story and allows us to partner with Him in bringing it to fullness in the earth. It's never based on how well we perform or our credibility. As believers, we are set apart because of forgiveness, not perfection. But because I hadn't yet embraced His grace in my own life, I had none to extend to His people. My heart was hard.

This one particular Sunday night, my mom and I had gone up to the church to drop David off for some sort of practice. When we pulled up, two of my friends saw me in the car and came over. They told me that the youth group was about to leave to go to a youth rally at another church in the area. After much hesitation on my part and much persuasion on theirs, I gave in. On the ride over, I remember thinking, "What have I gotten myself into?" I had no idea what to expect, but my expectations weren't very high. It would just come and go like any other night and I would go home the same as I came like I always did.

We walked inside and entered into a sanctuary full of youth groups from all over the area. Worship had already started, so we filed into a row of chairs near the back. As much as I did not want to engage, I have always loved music (especially worship music, even from the start) and I couldn't distract myself away from it. It drew me in and caught my attention note by note. The song "The Stand" by Hillsong was popular at the time and it was my current favorite. I had one of those classic "reason with God" moments and said, "Okay, if they do that song, I'll know I'm supposed to be here." I bet you can guess what song started right as the period hit the end of my sentence. In a moment, my heart shifted as I became aware of God's nearness right there in the middle of the unexpected.

After worship, one of the pastors went up and invited us into a time of prayer. He gave a couple of altar calls and when he got to the last one, something changed. I don't remember exactly what he said, but it was something along the lines of "getting real." He said, "If you're tired of playing church, get up here." My heart stood up before my body did, and my feet quickly followed down the aisle. I stood completely still in front of a crowd of people who knew nothing about me and a God who knew everything there was to know. In a moment, He reached down into my timeline and marked me exactly where I was.

To my left, a man stood at his seat in the front row. The pastor said to grab the hand of the person next to us, so the man grabbed my hand and the pastor began to pray. Although there was nothing magical about the words that were prayed or where I was standing, the Spirit of Jesus was among us and I felt the icy shell of my heart starting to melt in the warmth of His presence. When we were done praying, the man turned to me and said, "God has such good things planned for you. He is going to use you." In a moment, I was awakened to a sense of purpose I had never known before.

We all went back to our seats while the pastor introduced the speaker for the night. When I got to my chair and turned around to sit, I was shocked to see the man who had just been to my left standing on the platform. I don't remember his name or the details of his story, but I will never forget the confidence in his words of encouragement to me and the kindness in his eyes as he spoke them. I can't wait to see him again once we're in heaven and tell him how much that meant to me.

I did not go home the same as I came. My friends could instantly see the difference in me and they shared in my joy. I had never experienced anything like that and I thought that if it got any better, I might explode because I could hardly contain the life swelling inside of me. That night, I recognized who Jesus is and how much I needed Him. When I got home, I surrendered everything. I told God that I meant it when I went up to the altar. I was ready to get real. If this was what being a Christian is really like, I was in.

The next day at school, I was so excited to get to Bible class and tell my teacher that I gave my life to Jesus for real. I was so full of hope, and for the first time in a long time, I believed that my life held meaning. Things were looking up and I could not wait to start cleaning up the mess I'd made of myself and get back on track. It was like I had woken up from a dream in which I couldn't move or speak. I was no longer a puppet. There was now an eternity of freedom ahead of me and I was ready to jump right in.

I'm not over my depression. Days like today remind me. I don't want to feel like this. I feel like I can't control it and I hate it. I wish I didn't have this problem. I wish I were happy. I wish I could feel comfortable in my own skin. I wish when I look in the mirror I could smile and be proud of the person I've become, because I know I've made progress. I have days like today, though. They're hard days, days when I feel like I have no one to talk to, no one to trust, and no one that would understand. Days when I think, "Why shouldn't I cut? Nothing's getting better anyway." But I don't. I pray, and I know God hears me and loves me. But terrible things still happen, I still feel worthless, and I still have days like today. I still need help.

3
When the Hiding Place Shakes
He is Still There

If anything, the devil is consistent in character. No matter how appealing he makes something look or sound, no matter how good or bad your life gets, no matter how the times change, one thing never will: his desire is **always** to steal, kill, and destroy anything and everything he can gain access to (John 10:10). Now, it is important to understand that through the incredible gift of salvation by way of Jesus' death and resurrection, we have gained rights to complete freedom. Living free from fear is not a myth, healing did not end with the close of the New Testament, and overcoming is all-inclusive, not just for a lucky few. Because of what Jesus has done for us, these things are available to us in full measure, but one thing I have learned in my own process is that I cannot receive what I don't have room for.

One way I have learned to look at it is like this: I often found myself with my hands full. Along the way, I accumulated a heavy load: offenses from others, doubt from past experiences, brokenness from failed or unhealthy relationships, burdens from observing and empathizing with others in their own pain, and a myriad of other things.

It is painful to share your heart and be disagreed with or rejected. I didn't want anyone to see my feelings, so with my offences I built a barrier to keep a safe distance from that possibility. All the while, bitterness had plenty of room to grow on the inside.

When things don't work out the way you hoped or prayed they would, you can easily become disappointed in God and people, and if left untreated, this disappointment can turn into a welcome mat for doubt. However, I believe that disappointment and doubt can both serve as powerful tools when handled correctly. When we allow our disappointment and doubt to provoke questions and when we turn to the Lord for the answers, faith has room to flourish. The problem is when we allow disappointment to remain disappointment and doubt to remain doubt.

For a long time, I was stuck in this cycle. Hoping, praying, waiting, and being disappointed when I didn't see what *I* wanted to see. With each new hope for something, my hesitation grew as I remembered the disappointment from before and I started asking for less and less because it wasn't as risky. As if I needed to take it easy on God in case He couldn't do it. Doubt caused me to shrink back, close my eyes, and keep my mouth shut.

We need each other. In my opinion, God's will for our lives is not accomplished void of relationships. Even Jesus had a group of close friends during His ministry. But relationships are risky investments. We spend time, money, and energy. We put forth efforts, opinions, and trust as we share the deep things of our hearts. Sometimes vulnerability is given in return, but sometimes we bare ourselves to someone who doesn't value what we have shared. This response can bring a twinge of pain to our hearts, but without taking the risk, how would we ever discover those God has brought into our lives for His purposes? When we back away from the risk in fear of humiliation, rejection, or betrayal, we rob ourselves of the opportunity to grow, learn, and experience the joy and sorrow of doing life with one another. This is the beauty of the Body.

Because I had felt such pain in relationships, especially at church, I had a brokenness in my heart that crippled me. I wanted to hide and keep to myself. I was convinced loneliness was the only safe place. Perhaps it is safe, but it is lonely. I didn't want to be alone, but I didn't want to get hurt, so I put locks on all my doors and buried the keys with their painful memories.

There were a few people I was close to. I loved them very much and I knew they loved me too. I liked to listen and I genuinely cared about what they were feeling and facing, but there is a fine line between compassion and compiling. I was a big compiler; I took the hurts, frustrations, and anxieties of others and stuffed them into my own backpack as my responsibility to carry. It is never our job to absorb other people's burdens; instead we are to bear with one another, encourage one another, and bring our concerns to the Lord in prayer (see Galatians 6:1-5, 1 Corinthians 12:26).

So here is the image: I was behind walls that I had built up, surrounded by once beautiful gardens now infested with bitter weeds of doubt and disappointment. I backed myself into a corner. I had my eyes closed and mouth shut, hesitating to speak or look up. Even if I did call out for help, I had locked all the doors and buried the keys, so no one could get inside. In my chest was a heavy heart and on my shoulders was a load even heavier, far too heavy for one person to carry. Yet it was my home, all I had known for a long time. Although I recognized that it was a dark and miserable place, I was comfortable. I had developed a pattern, a routine, a lifestyle in that habitat; and changing it meant changing my whole world.

"Behold, I stand at the door and knock." I heard His voice. I suddenly became aware that He had come to respond to the yearning in my heart that I had tried to ignore and fill with other things. All my doors were locked and He was on the outside, but He had the key. He had the key, and yet He didn't pry. He waited patiently for my welcoming.

That night at the youth rally, I finally welcomed Him into my life. He saw all of it. Nothing was ever hidden from Him, even when He was on the outside. He knew me fully from the beginning and saw every bit of dirt and darkness, yet He came to me in my corner and embraced me. His love looked right past all of my circumstances and came in close. He didn't start picking up my mess right away and taking all my pain. He came to me first. Something really beautiful about our salvation is that now we have the Holy Spirit and we get to clean it up together (2 Corinthians 6:1-2; John 14:16-18). As we do, we get to discover His heart for us in the process.

When I gave my whole heart to Jesus that night and surrendered myself to Him, I invited Him into my whole life – every part. Sometimes I resisted Him, but my desire was to let Him in past my discomfort. You see, I expected my life to be all better after that. I was ready for God to pick up all the pieces and fill me with joy and hope and make me totally free, but that's not always how it works.

I was holding onto so much fear, pride, and pain that I had nowhere to put the love and peace He wanted to give me. Before I could receive any of that and experience real, lasting change in my life, we had to clear out the old and make room for the new. I remember distinctly how He used to tell me, "We have to deconstruct in order to reconstruct." We had to tear down the walls, uproot those weeds, unlock the doors, open my eyes, and let go of all the things I was holding onto. It was not a quick process.

I rode the spiritual high of the youth rally for a while, but I didn't have the truth I needed to sustain this awakening. I was going to church and learning in Bible class, and it was all truth, but it was only information to me at the time. It had to become real, living revelation rooted deep in my heart in order for me to start walking in the fullness of my freedom. I had to really believe it. I think this is where a lot of people get stuck or give up. It's easy to hop from conference to conference or survive off of hyped-up events, but what happens when it's just you and Jesus?

If we don't get the truth laid out as our firm foundation, we are building on sand (see Matthew 7:24-27 for the details). I was recently discussing this concept with a friend of mine and he said something that completely shifted my perspective. I was asking him about his interpretation of the storms and rock and sand, and he said so profoundly that sand is just fragments of rock: just bits and pieces of truth, not sturdy enough to withstand the waves. I had been building on sand.

As the hype and excitement wore off, I realized that I still had the same pain in my heart, I was still bitter, and I still needed a whole lot of help. I needed the Holy Spirit to walk me through forgiveness, letting go, and believing the truth. He did, but it took some time because the sudden dryness startled me. I went from feeling refreshed and vibrant to feeling like I was stranded in the wilderness somewhere, desperate for water. I wondered where God was and why I didn't feel happy anymore. In fact, I began to spiral downward and out of control.

My life was suddenly caught up in the tension of choosing whether to continue trusting God and pushing through or to return to my old place of comfort, hidden and afraid. My relationships were falling apart, my family was stirred with conflict, and I was bombarded with lies from the old voice that I had once given control over my thoughts and emotions. The devil was not happy that Someone else had come into the picture. He may not mind a bunch of people becoming Christians, but one thing satan has no tolerance for is a bunch of believers being awakened to the truth: that he is eternally a defeated loser and has absolutely NO power over those who are in Christ Jesus (1 John 5:18).

The devil flung his fiery darts my way with a vengeance, but I didn't know how to stand on my own yet. I hadn't opened up to anyone who could help me stand firm, not even my parents. These are the moments when it is vital to have each other, but I was alone and afraid. I wanted to believe Jesus, I wanted to trust His Word, but I struggled. Every day was a fight and the lies got louder and louder, but I cried out to God and I chose to turn to Him.

I began to journal my heart out. I read Psalms about David's despair and cried because I so desperately wanted to hear the Lord's response as David did; I was still learning to recognize His voice. At the time I felt like He had left me to fight on my own, but when I read back through those journal entries, I think He must have been teaching me. He was giving me opportunities to learn to run to Him instead of back into my hiding. I failed often, but His love for me never did.

This went on for a couple of months. I had started opening up because I knew I needed help and I decided to take the risk to share my pain with a few people. I was starting to let go of past hurts and disappointments, so I finally had an open space. This moment of void holds a crucial decision for us. Here we have the choice of either letting God come and fill our emptiness or filling it with something else. Allowing God to fill those places requires trust and patience, but our human nature can't stand the discomfort, and as a result, the temptation arises to find something else to fill those places as quickly as we can (Matthew 26:41). The flesh loves comfort.

There was one day in particular where I had to make this choice. A friend of mine said something at school that really hurt me. The Lord was helping me break down my walls of offence, so I had to decide whether to build the walls back up or turn to His truth for the strength I needed to let it go. Something to keep in mind is that the enemy will always take advantage of this moment as well. He will do anything he can to get you to turn back to the darkness and isolation of your hiding.

Sitting in the classroom, I tried to be strong. I tried to hold it together, but the lies exaggerated my pain and convinced me not only that what my friend said was true, but also that I was worthless and that I deserved the pain. I believed I was a burden and that no one wanted to hear it. They had their own lives to worry about and I was just getting in the way. I was the negative one, the downer. Who wants to have that person hanging around? I believed that I was the one ruining everything and that it was my fault my life was falling apart. Everything was blown way out of proportion and I hated myself as I sat there accepting all of this as truth.

I asked my teacher if I could go to the restroom. I had to get out, I had to do something. I felt like I was going out of control. I walked down the hall and into the ladies' room in our carpeted gym where I knew no one would find me. I was devastated and furious. I wanted to cry, longing for some sort of release, but it didn't come. I took matters into my own hands. I didn't stop and wait for

God, I didn't turn to Him. Instead I found something sharp in my purse and before I could realize what I had done, my wrist was bleeding. I sat there in shock and stared in disbelief at my self-destruction. As quickly as relief came, it left and was replaced by shame. What had I done? I knew I couldn't hide this for long, and even when it healed, there would be a mark constantly reminding me of my failure that day.

I still have faded reminders on my wrists today, but now they are precious to me because I can look back and see that every time I found myself in the same regret, He came into my corner and embraced me. And He kept coming, even the second and third and fourth and tenth time. He was always there. He always will be.

4
Bittersweet Heartbreak & All It Exposes

When I think back to high school, I am quickly reminded why I don't often think back to high school. Yes, I made plenty of good memories with friends and family that I love, had some great experiences, and grew a lot as a person, but I can confidently say that I would never want to go back. I have had my fill of adolescent ups and downs, heartbreak, and drama. I had my first real boyfriend, first real breakup, first job, went to my first concert, got my first tattoo, and several other memorable firsts. A lot of them were good and I am thankful for the memories, but others were very painful.

Even as I started opening up to people more, it was difficult to trust. It was still hard for me to share what I was going through with the people around me, fearing that they might not care; and even if they did care they probably wouldn't understand.

As I transitioned into the last four years at my private school, I counted down the days to freedom. I was ready for graduation on the first day of my freshman year, thinking that once I got out of there, things would finally fall into place and I could move on from all the struggles and pain I was feeling at the time. However, all of these things (the fear, the anxiety, the eating disorder, the cutting, and all the rest) were baggage that I carried around with me everywhere I went.

When I was in ninth grade, I became interested in a boy a year above me. We were in the same math class and I noticed that he seemed to be interested in me too. This was a new feeling for me and I didn't quite know what to do with it. Every day I walked outside to our portable buildings and up the short flight of stairs that led to our classroom. Some days I would wait outside and stall for a bit, using every moment of the break in between classes wisely. I would think carefully about what to say and take a deep breath before opening the door that I knew he was just on the other side of. We talked and laughed and wrote notes, and I was quickly falling for him. It wasn't long before he expressed his feelings to me.

I was excited, giddy, and terrified all at once. I had never experienced anything like this before. I knew that a relationship with this guy would mean more vulnerability, honesty, and open communication, and that made me nervous. He had found me in the midst of a full-blown eating disorder and I was still cutting. He didn't know about it at first, but I was afraid that if he saw what I was dealing with, he might change his mind about me and find someone else that was prettier and had less issues. But the fact that he still pursued me made me feel valuable.

Over the next few months, we developed a closer friendship and I started to trust him. I told him a little bit about what I was going through and shared my feelings with him, and much to my surprise, he responded with vulnerability of his own. I didn't expect for him to care as much as he did. I had talked to people about my struggles before, but usually they didn't know what to say. I didn't blame them for not understanding, but after a while, I stopped anticipating a response at all.

With him it was different. He took the time to listen to me and offered encouragement where he could. He went out of his way to make me feel special, bringing gifts to surprise me at school and writing me sweet notes about how beautiful I was to him and how glad he was to know me. We were able to be there for each other and I was so happy to have someone who cared about me that way. It was exciting! I was overjoyed when I arrived at school on my fifteenth birthday only to be greeted by his smile and an invitation to be his girlfriend. I happily said yes and we began our new journey together.

Each time I remembered I was a girlfriend, my stomach swirled in knots and tumbled butterflies that hardly ever settled down when I was around him. I couldn't believe I had found someone who saw who I really was and still chose me. I was thrilled to be chosen by someone like him, a boy that several other girls had liked and dated. He caught everyone's eye, and yet somehow I ended up being the one who caught his at the time. He told me I was beautiful and I tried to believe it, but there was a hesitation in the back of my mind that sprang up any time I was complimented.

I constantly compared myself to other girls. Even though my boyfriend said I was pretty, I was tempted to believe he was only saying it because that's what boyfriends say, and I always found my way back to the train of thought that led me straight into discouragement. As months went by and the early relationship bliss faded, I found that I was left with the same pain all over again. The relationship I thought would ease my insecurity ended up amplifying it, and now I was striving to be "good enough" again.

My boyfriend never once told me to act differently or look a certain way. He never held up a picture of what he considered "the perfect body" or made a list of requirements for me to fulfill as his girlfriend, but in my mind I felt like I had to do more, be more attractive, and earn his affection. I was so afraid of losing him that I became consumed with being perfect again.

In this new kind of vulnerability, I was exhausted with trying to cover the parts of my heart that were now exposed. As we got closer, I presented pieces of myself to him in timidity, wondering if showing him the next piece would be too much and would result in rejection. As you can imagine, this caused conflict. I felt like a burden, so I acted like one. I wore myself out and I'm sure he felt just as worn trying to prove to me that he meant what he said. To him, it was like talking to a wall; for me, it was just too good to be true.

There was something in me that fought back when he tried to love me, as if my heart was refusing to take the risk of letting anyone come any closer. I felt like my insides were panicking, like I was treading water somewhere in the middle of the ocean with my feet miles from the safety and comfort of the sand somewhere beneath. No one had ever seen this much of me before and I felt paralyzed. Our relationship started to fall apart and eventually ended in the first loss that truly broke me.

All I saw was the bad. All I felt was the pain. Every night I cried, missing him and hating myself for ruining such a good thing. I started eating less and cutting more because of the grief. I did it because I believed I deserved the pain; I believed it was all my fault. I could have kept him, I could have been enough, I could have... All I could remember was the times I should have just been myself, should have just spoken up, should have just been honest. He wanted to be there for me, but I tried to carry it all on my own again. I felt bad for involving him in my mess and making him go through it with me, but I kept forgetting that he chose to. He wanted to because he chose me.

I treated Jesus the same way, and I felt bad every time I confessed another sin or shortcoming. By now I was aware that I was back to believing lies. I had been reading my Bible and journaling the whole time, and I knew better because He spoke to me. I was able to hear His voice because I had learned to recognize His heart, but I let the pain overtake me and I ran back into my corner as depression set in.

Thankfully, the Lord knew how to reach me. He always knows exactly where to find us. When I was in eighth grade, a new youth pastor, Josh Boice, came to our church with his wife, Leah. I was so excited because she was a psychologist, something I dreamed of being one day. She has a heart for helping hurting people and I was so grateful to have her around. She ended up teaching at the school and

I got to be in a couple of her classes through the years. My favorite one was of course, Psychology.

Our school was very small and didn't have many electives to choose from, but they decided to add that one after the Boices came, during my sophomore year. One perk of offering a new elective at such a small school was that it was also a small class. To be more specific, there were three of us: me, another student, and Mrs. Boice. It was really special to me that I had those days with her.

The other student was two years older than me (a senior at the time) and sometimes had other stuff going on, so when he had to miss class, I got to spend some quality time with Leah. Figuring she would probably understand what I was going through better than most people, I asked if I could talk to her about what I had been dealing with the past few years. She listened intently and was patient with me while I vented, cried, and let her see into my broken heart. I explained the way I was feeling to her and she gave me honest advice, molded by the truth God had revealed to her through her own experiences. Although she sympathized with me, she never let me make excuses for giving into thought processes that would keep me bound by lies. She taught me to keep leaning on the Lord, trusting Him as my Constant, and to stand on His truth. She encouraged me and loved me, and she stood with me in the fight.

I don't know what I would have done without Leah during that time in my life. I know it was no coincidence that we both ended up at that school and church when we did. God's timing is perfect, and I believe He planned on crossing our paths from the beginning. He knew I would need the wisdom and love He had given her to share, and He also knew that she would be reminded there of how the pain and struggles from her own story were now being used for good and for His glory.

For a long time, Leah was the only person I opened up to. I felt safe sharing with her because I knew she saw where I was coming from, and never saw me differently on the other side of my honesty. She also had a deeper understanding of why we sometimes feel the things we do when we hurt, and that helped me process my feelings as well. On one hand, I seemed to be getting better and the wounds were starting to heal. I was learning so much from her and growing stronger in the Lord; but on the other hand, I was feeling like any time I did try to stand up, another wave came crashing in to knock me back down. I felt so weak, like I had nothing left to give. I didn't want to give up, but I didn't understand why it was so hard.

There is a quote from a book called *Captivating* by John and Stasi Eldredge that has stuck with me ever since I first read it many years ago:

You are passionately loved by the God of the universe. You are passionately hated by His enemy.[1]

It is crucial that we understand this: Just as God has a plan for our lives, so does our enemy. He is "out to get us." When we are getting ahold of the truth of God's Word and discovering our identity in Him, satan will stop at nothing to be sure we are hindered from believing that truth. However, he has no new tricks up his sleeve. There is nothing he can do that he hasn't tried before. He cannot read our minds or control anything that we haven't handed over to him (knowingly or unknowingly); he just has lots of experience with humankind and has become skilled in how to read us and play the cards to his advantage.

I have heard it said that one of satan's greatest tools is deceiving people into thinking he doesn't exist. He's done a good job of convincing us. He likes for us to think that people and circumstances are our enemies, when in fact, he is the puppet master behind it all. In her *Armor of God* Bible study, Priscilla Shirer speaks to this concept with beautiful clarity:

> Your real enemy – the devil – wants you to ignore the spiritual reality behind the physical one. Because as long as you're focused on what you can see with your physical eyes, he can continue to run rampant underneath the surface. The more you disregard him, the more damage he is free to do. The enemy may be invisible, but he is not fictional. He is very real, and very persistent, waging war against us constantly.[2]

So often we get distracted by what's going on out here where we can see. We blame our disappointments and pain and failures on other people and we say, "If only I hadn't been born this way or raised like that," or "If I had been treated differently..." And all the while, satan sits laughing, pleased with his deceptive work. We take the bait. In the same Bible study, Priscilla paints a picture using an illustration where children at a carnival are playing a homemade version of whack-a-mole in which some people are sitting behind a curtain raising puppeted hands for the children to hit back down. She said that one child in particular walked up to the game, looked it over in curiosity, and had to get to the bottom of what was going on. The child walked right up and pulled down the curtain to expose the people hiding beneath. They were the ones moving the puppets, the real culprits.

How often do we wear ourselves out trying to keep those pesky moles out of sight? We try and try to keep our problems below the surface and have it all together, but all the while we are dealing with branches instead of the root. For a long time, I was cutting away branches thinking that it would alleviate the heaviness I carried. Although I was relieved temporarily, branches can grow back, and new branches continue to grow as long as the root is intact. This is exactly what our enemy wants us to do: waste our time ripping down leaves and rotten branches, thinking the bad stuff will just go away, but until we get to the root issue, it will continue to produce filth and pain in our lives.

During my sophomore year, Leah and I did a lot of digging. She loved me as I opened up the deep places in my heart that I had kept locked and hidden for as long as I could remember. Like being in a dark room for a long time and then walking out into the sunlight, those places were sensitive and raw as I adjusted my vision to see clearly. It was painful, but brought such freedom.

The deeper we go, the more appealing it sounds to give up, because of course the devil's desire is to keep us wrapped up in the fibers of bitter roots and darkness. But thank God, He is light. Darkness is not the opposite of light; it is the absence of it. There is no power in darkness, for Light has stripped it all away. The power is in the light's source, and where there is light, darkness cannot exist.

Little by little, Light was breaking into my world one hiding place at a time.

Sometimes I think the world would be better off without me. No more tears from the stupid girl that's way too sensitive and emotional. All she does is cry and wallow in stupid self-pity. She knows the thoughts are lies, but they overpower her. They want to kill her. They want her to kill herself. Her friends wouldn't have to listen to her whine; her poor boyfriend wouldn't suffer anymore... He's the one she hurts the most. He deserves better. That's what she's afraid of: that he'll decide to take a better offer. There are plenty of beautiful, carefree girls that don't have her problems. If she could, she would run away. Far, far away from this body. She desperately wants to be better. She's in agony because she knows she's at fault.

5
Get Me Out of Here

They say that sometimes things have to get worse before they can get better. Sometimes we have to hit rock bottom before we realize we've been standing on sand. That's how it happened for me, at least. I picked up some momentum as I spiraled downward and I felt like my world was spinning out of control as I waited for some sort of end. Day and night, I was taunted by a voice in my head that said I would never be enough. I followed lies down a path that led me far away from reality and even farther from the truth. I felt like I was going crazy and I didn't know what to do.

Depression settled over me and I felt trapped. I hated how hard it was for me to be happy. It was almost embarrassing at times, because as a Christian I wanted to represent Christ and the hope and life He gives. But how could I when I felt like my own life was hanging on by only a thread?

I spent nights crying out for Jesus to come save me and heal my heart. I put my trust in Him, but where was He? I needed Him more than ever. I felt like my friends and family were getting tired of hearing about my problems and I didn't want to be a burden anymore. Even some teachers pointed out that I had a bad attitude and my dad just said I needed to stop being so negative. If only it were that easy.

I was not just moping around and whining about how bad my life was all the time. I was fighting to hold on, no longer running from my pain, but embracing it and trying to face it. I knew that was the only way to get free, but it was not easy. Every day, I was bombarded with temptations to continue cutting. Every time I opened up to someone, I was tempted to take their lack of understanding as rejection and remain a slave to disappointment. Every time I looked in the mirror, I wanted to love myself. I wanted to be happy and free and enjoy life, but something in me would just not let go.

Several of my relationships suffered in the process. I don't blame them for not understanding the depression, because most people who have not experienced it firsthand just don't know. It is a heavy burden, but no one who is fighting it should have to fight alone.[1]

During my sophomore year of high school, I felt incredibly misunderstood and alone. It was as if no matter how many colors I combined, I could never paint a clear picture of what was going on inside for someone else to see. I didn't know how to explain it, and I was often left feeling defeated and at times even invisible.

One night in September 2010, a friend who was on the cheerleading squad with me was having a birthday party. She and I were close, so I went early to hang out with her and help set up. We were both excited for the party and couldn't wait for everyone else to get there. Soon they arrived and the night was in full swing.

Some of the other cheerleaders came, and my ex-boyfriend was there too. It was hard enough having the same friend group and seeing each other at school everyday. At the time I was still trying to get over the breakup, so when one of the other cheerleaders came over to me and asked to talk with me privately, my mind immediately went to the worst. I began to draw my own conclusions as we walked around the corner into an area where no one else was around. She started off by saying that she was glad we were friends, but that I couldn't change things. She and my ex-boyfriend liked each other and wanted to be together. She said she knew it would hurt me, but that he didn't want to be with me anymore, and that I just needed to accept that.

She walked away and I fell completely silent, shocked by a reality I had been avoiding for a while. I had seen it coming, but denied it hoping a friendship would take precedence over a fling that would most likely fade as quickly as it had started. I was devastated, and although it may seem petty now, that moment caused something inside of me to crack. It was the final straw the broke the camel's back.

I watched as she walked away, turning the corner to rejoin the party on the other side of the wall. On my side of the wall I now sat on the floor by myself, crying between two old vending machines. I felt utterly helpless and out of control, like I was falling thousands of feet, anticipating the impact of a crash landing without having any idea how long I had before I hit the pavement. The pain shook my body in tremors from the deepest part of my bones and I could hardly breathe. It was another anxiety attack, which I was used to by now, but this one was much worse. I couldn't stop it or calm myself down. My breaths came shorter and shorter and the room started to spin.

It didn't take long for some friends to realize that I was missing from the party and to come looking for me. I was horrified by the display of emotions that I was no longer able to hide and I didn't want them to find me. Everything that I had fought so hard to keep out of sight was coming to the surface and I wanted to get out. I felt absolutely raw and stripped bare. Why was this happening to me? Why here? Why now?

This was the exact thing I had dreaded: for them to see the real me, what was really going on inside. I was convinced that they would be disgusted with what they saw and leave. I wanted to run away and pretend it wasn't real. I couldn't believe what was happening, and I couldn't believe that someone I had trusted was actually okay with walking away knowing the pain she had inflicted.

My friends came over to where I was and asked what had happened and if I was okay. I could hardly come up with words to answer them. They saw that I was panicking and asked if they should call an ambulance. At that point I realized how stupid and completely insane I must have looked for them to want to call an ambulance. I was mortified. I wanted to die.

The thought had entered my mind more frequently over the past few months as the depression got thicker around and inside of me:

Would it really make that much of a difference if I wasn't here? Honestly, I think it might be better because then the people I love wouldn't have to worry about me anymore. I'm more of a burden anyway. I just cause people pain. I just ruin good things and annoy people with my problems. And I wouldn't have to feel trapped by this depression anymore or starve myself and cut to feel better. Maybe this is what's best...

The rest of the night was a blur. I stayed at the party and went through the motions, trying to celebrate with my friend and put on a happy face for her birthday the best that I could, one last performance. I didn't want to ruin the night more than I already had. I knew she was worried about me. I tried to be present and engage in what was going on, but I honestly didn't care. Apathy set in. My mind was fixed on one thing and I couldn't wait to leave.

When I got home, I went straight to my room. A dark cloud hemmed me in as I turned off the lights and closed the door behind me. I shut down all my mind's systems and emotions, and I said goodbye to my memories one by one. I sat in silence, taking in a few last breaths and considerations. Was this the right thing to do? I didn't leave myself any room to think about it because I had made up my mind and it was too late to turn around. I had made a fool of myself and was sure that no one would be surprised in the morning. I knew my family would be sad, but I didn't want to think about them either. I loved them so much and I just wanted them to be happy. They spent so much time worrying about me and putting up with me. Once they got over the initial shock and grief, they would be able to get back to life as usual without the extra stress I had caused for so long.

I thought about God. I tried not to, but I couldn't deny that He was seeing it all, which made me feel so ugly and disappointing. I didn't really know it then, and I certainly didn't feel it, but He was right there with me in the last moments. Although darkness had made me feel comfortable with dying in that room, persuading me that it was the only escape, Jesus was still holding onto me.

But I decided to give in. I decided that suicide was the only way to bring relief to everyone, myself included. Tears streamed down my face as I accepted what I was about to do. I closed my eyes to turn off the world around me for the last time and darkness thought it had won. But the next morning I woke up – alive.

6
Waking Up: No More Hiding

I woke up in shock, my mind in a haze as I tried to gather my memories of the night before. Tiny rays of morning sunlight poked through my window and informed me that I had somehow made it to the next day. I was not exactly thrilled when I realized this and looked at the clock to find that not only was it time to get up, but it was Sunday and we would be leaving for church soon. Great.

I was so confused. I couldn't remember what had happened. All I could remember was crying, thinking about what I was about to do, and then waking up. I'm sure my body was exhausted from the stress and lack of nutrition, but I didn't remember falling asleep or even being tired. I tried not to think about it too much, because I knew if my parents saw me acting strange they would start asking questions. I didn't want to talk about it. I didn't want to be awake. I didn't want to deal with this – not today, not ever.

On our way to church, Mom and Dad told us that we were going out for lunch to celebrate their anniversary. I had forgotten all about that. I began to think that maybe it was a good thing my plans didn't work out the night before. I would've hated to ruin their anniversary with the constant reminder of what I had done. Thinking about it all, I got frustrated because I wished I had either gone through with it sooner or could get over it now and just be happy. I was so heavy with hopelessness and my chest felt hollow even though the ache in my heart throbbed like it would burst at any moment. But I could not let that happen again. People had seen enough, so in an effort to spare them all I ran back into my hiding. If I could just hold on a little longer, maybe I could figure this thing out.

I sat through the service and gave a halfhearted attempt to care about what was going on, but my mind was disconnected from my surroundings. I wanted to be alone and I didn't want to care anymore. At this point, I felt nothing and I was okay with that. If I were going to live, I would do it in the safety of my walls. I may not ever be happy, but if it meant not having to feel the pain, I reasoned that it would be worth it to forfeit the chance of feeling the love too.

When the service ended, I went out into the hallway so I could avoid talking to anyone. I waited there for my parents while they were talking to some of their friends. It was taking them a while, but I figured they were just catching up or discussing upcoming events like usual. They finally came, but my brother and sister weren't with them. I just wanted to go to lunch and get it over with so we could move on with the day. Why couldn't they just cooperate and come on? I asked my parents where they were and they told me that David and Kuri were going home with their friends. I didn't understand what was going on. We had plans to go to lunch as a family and now my siblings were skipping out? Before I could ask why, my Mom told me that we were going to talk to Leah.

I was speechless. What could we possibly have to talk about with Leah today? My heart was racing as we walked into the little room Josh used as his youth office. Leah was one of few that knew about what I was going through, and she was the only one I had shared the depth of my struggles with besides God. I was afraid, but I tried to stay composed.

We all sat down, Leah in Josh's desk chair to my right and my parents across from me. I looked at Leah and then at my parents. My dad seemed serious, but not upset, maybe just deep in thought. Beside him, my mom looked concerned, like she was seeing something she hadn't before or perhaps had seen and denied. I waited for someone to tell me what in the world was going on. My mom looked at me with tears in her eyes, and her words came desperately hoping that my response would prove her suspicions untrue. She knew.

She asked if I was cutting myself. All at once, the feelings I had tried to keep at a distance rushed in and I was filled with rage, fear, shame, and total humiliation. I looked at Leah, wishing she could get me out of this uncomfortable situation somehow; but I knew I couldn't lie or cover it up anymore. I had been wearing jackets and long-sleeved shirts every day so my parents wouldn't find out, and I had tried so hard to keep it all together and get back to normal again. Leah had been encouraging me over the past few months as I tried to stop cutting, but as my youth pastor, teacher, and confidant, she was obligated to tell my parents if I was continuing to put myself at risk.

I hadn't cut myself in a few weeks, but after the party I gave in again. Leah didn't know about that yet though, so who would have told? My mom explained that one of my friends found out and told her mom because she was worried about me, and then that mom told my mom last night. I couldn't believe it. While I was in my room planning to end my life, my mom was finding out and most likely crying out to God in her own room.

Although there was a slight sense of relief in the exposure, I felt betrayed. I didn't want my parents to know, and I didn't want to admit that I wasn't okay, because I didn't want to be a disappointment. I was still striving to be good enough – for them, for myself, for God. Now I couldn't hide. I was sure that my parents would be upset with me, angry for lying and hurt that I didn't tell them. I said I was sorry and looked at them anticipating disapproval and punishment, but all I received in return for the truth of my brokenness was compassion. My mom's eyes were no longer filled with fear, but with mercy and sympathy. My dad and I weren't very close, but I could tell that even though he didn't understand, he wanted to make sure I was protected and provided for. That was always his intention and I realized that when he asked me what they could do to help.

I never expected a response like that. I was sure they would be disappointed in me and embarrassed that they had a kid with so many issues, but all they did that day and every day before and after was love me. My mom said that they would do whatever it took to help me get better. Leah suggested that I see a counselor. The thought of opening up to someone new was scary and I dreaded it, but I knew that if I were going to get through this, it would take some more discomfort and exposure.

I felt bad that my parents would have to spend the money because I felt like such a burden already, but my mom helped me understand that I was not a burden, and she assured me that they would much rather put money towards helping me get better than planning my funeral. Now that they knew, they promised they would stand with me in the fight. For the next few years, they did exactly that.

When we finished talking with Leah, we went to lunch. It had been a while since I had some quality time with my parents, and I didn't realize how much I needed it. They didn't pry, but I answered the questions they did ask and tried to open up enough to help them understand what I was going through. I shared with them about the depression and cutting, but I decided to keep the eating disorder to myself. I had caused them enough pain for one day and I figured I could just handle it on my own or in counseling.

On the way home, I thought about the events that had transpired within the last 24 hours: What a whirlwind of emotions. What a tremendous amount of grace God had shown me when all I did was block Him out. What an unexpected opportunity to open up and begin healing with my family by my side. And what a journey I had ahead of me. Somehow in all these things, God was moving. Every time I took a wrong turn and thought He had abandoned me, He was busy working behind the scenes, paving a detour for me so I could get back onto the right path. God never got tired of redeeming and restoring me; and what I thought was the end of my story was only the beginning.

7

Reconnecting / The Grace That Stills the Striving Heart

Have you ever gone to the movies to see a sequel with someone who hasn't seen the first one? You try to pay attention, completely drawn in by the intensity of each plot twist, eagerly waiting to see what will happen next and how the cliffhangers of the previous movie will be resolved; but all the while, the one you are sharing the moment with is lost. They can see what's happening now, and they might be able to connect some dots here and there and figure out the characters and the scenario, but they don't know the background and all the details that shaped the present circumstances in the story. You try to answer their questions and give quick recaps throughout to get them up to speed, but even if you were to take the time to catch them up on all that they had missed, the movie would still be playing and there would only be more to catch up on when you finished.

That's kind of how I viewed counseling in the beginning. I was very skeptical, and I wasn't looking forward to talking to a stranger and filling her in on all the things she wasn't there for the past fifteen years of my life. Not to mention, I knew she probably wasn't going to be there for the next fifteen years, so I figured, "What's the point?" I was hesitant to say the least.

There was so much going on in my life that it would be several sessions before my counselor and I could finally discuss the problems I currently had. I thought it would take forever for me to start feeling better. There was a lot of backtracking, a lot of researching family history and identifying triggers. It was all helpful, but in my mind I was there for a solution. I wanted a practical answer for why it was so hard for me to be happy. I wanted a quick fix so I could move on.

I went into my counselor's office every week wondering if we would make any progress. I didn't open up to her very much, so we didn't get very far. I know she tried, but she kept saying that we just needed to find ways to help me cope better. But I didn't want to cope with my depression; I wanted to get through it. I wanted to be free, if that was even possible.

Months passed and I started to open up more about my suicidal thoughts, depression, and anxiety (still keeping the eating disorder my secret). Although it was nice to let out some of what I had kept bottled up for years, I felt like it was only show-and-tell, not letting go and healing. I felt like we hit a wall and couldn't dig any deeper. I felt misunderstood.

The desire to get better did not come naturally or easily to me. The way I saw it, the brokenness I carried in my heart and fought to keep concealed was simply normal. My twisted thought processes were destructive and laced with lies, but they were comfortable and all I had known for years. To me, getting better was a feeling similar to leaving the house you grew up in. The pain of separation often tempted me to quietly return to my hiding where no one could see what was actually going on under my skin: I was trapped beneath the wreckage and I couldn't get out on my own.

Healing requires humility and courage. Since I cared so much about what people thought, I had a hard time letting go of the image I had been working so hard to achieve. I thought that if my friends found out I was going to counseling, they would think I was crazy or something. It was pride that made it so difficult to choose to loosen my grip. I say it's a choice because to be honest, it is. If I had not been intentional about getting up and seeking help, I would still be trapped like a bird sitting on a perch inside a cage with an open door, unaware of my own wings – my ability to soar, to find safety and freedom. Healing is much more attainable than we are led to believe.

After counseling sessions, my mom would pick me up. She always asked me how it went and I would usually respond with a general answer, feeling bad that I wasn't better yet, but trying to make an effort ("fake it until you make it," right? Well, it never really works out that way). I could tell that it was wearing on her to watch my discouragement settle in. One day she asked me if the counseling was helping at all. I took a deep breath, hesitant to tell her the truth that I wasn't making much progress. I expected disappointment once again, but she lovingly nodded her head in longing compassion. I know she wished she could take my pain away.

My mom has always had a keen awareness of spiritual warfare. I remember growing up, before my family was really even growing spiritually, how she would remind us that we have a real enemy that is always trying to keep us from fulfilling God's purpose for our lives. After that talk in the car, she brought up the idea of going to a Christian counselor instead. I agreed that it would probably be more effective to have someone who better understood the spiritual side of things.

Seeing a Christian counselor was much better. I knew I would have to go through all the background information again and spill my guts to yet another person who would be in my life only temporarily, but I knew it was what would have to be done if I was ever going to move past this.

Slowly, but surely, there was improvement. As I opened up to my new counselor and we talked about the Lord, I started to feel more comfortable.

She reminded me who God says I am – the truth straight from His Word – and she encouraged me to continue to remind myself of that truth when I was tempted to believe the lies and get sucked back into mindsets shaped by hopelessness. I gradually began to feel lighter as I surrendered my heavy load to Jesus daily, and by the time my sophomore year was over, I was feeling more optimistic than I had in years.

The summer before my junior year, I reconnected with a good friend of mine. We were best friends throughout elementary school, but grew apart when she changed schools in eighth grade. She is one of those friends that no matter where you both are in life, you can get together and pick up right where you left off, as if there was never any space between. We hung out all summer long and most of junior year. At the time, she was going to a youth group in the area called Jesus Generation and she always told me about how great it was. She invited me to come with her one Wednesday, so I did. I will never forget it.

When we left, I couldn't stop thinking about how different it was. I loved my youth group and church, but there was something about the environment at JG that captivated me. The people there were so full of life and joy, and they welcomed me in like family. They were excited about God and wanted to know Him more. During the worship time, the band created opportunities for the whole room to engage and encounter Jesus. The prayers were genuine and the message was powerful. I wanted more.

I knew there were people in my school and youth group who were sincerely seeking the Lord and I was so blessed to learn from them and grow with them there. The difficulty is that when you go to a Christian school, especially one that's under the same roof as your church, it's easy to fake it. Students at the school are automatically assumed by most to be believers. However, if you have been to Christian school or are familiar with them, you know that unfortunately this is usually not the case. It's safe to say that we had the same kinds of drama and misconduct you would find at any other school. The difference is that in public school, a lot of Christians stand out; at our school, everyone went to Bible class and chapel, and we all looked the same.

What appealed to me about JG was that the people who were there *wanted* to be there. It wasn't required or forced; it was their choice. Regardless of whether they actually cared or applied the truth of each lesson to their lives, the fact is that they made the effort. They weren't perfect people and they didn't try to be, nor did they need to be. They were just real people going through real seasons of life, and they wanted Jesus. They wanted to be there, and I wanted to be there with them. Eventually I was going every single week, even when my friend who invited me stopped going.

The student leaders in the youth group loved and encouraged me, and we quickly became friends. One of the worship team members, Puckett, discovered that I liked to sing. I led worship at school for chapel on Wednesdays and sometimes sang in the choir for Christmas services and special events at church, but when he asked if I would audition for their team, I was afraid. I had never done anything more than sing songs, but I knew from watching them each week that it was so much more than music. It was true worship, a connection with God that they invited the rest of the room into. I felt insecure and so unqualified, but the youth pastor and team assured me that I already had everything I needed inside of me. During my time there, they challenged me as I grew and they called out the potential in me.

Puckett taught me a lot about worship. He and another leader, Martin, made time to answer my questions and teach me about what real relationship with Jesus is like. We had lots of talks about the Holy Spirit and what it means to follow His lead. During that time in my life, I began to learn that it's not up to me to have it all together or make things happen.

For most of my life, I have struggled to wrap my mind around the concept of grace, which is ironic because that's exactly what my name means; but I don't think that's a coincidence. It was a fight for my identity. Because I had aimed to be "perfect" for so long, my default thought processes became entirely motivated by doing good and striving to be good enough. I was constantly trying to measure up to the standards I had set for myself and believed others had set for me as well. It was that never-ending cycle again.

A few summers ago, my family took a vacation to the beach. I was sitting on the balcony one morning, looking out to the sea and watching the tide roll in, crash against itself, and retreat back to the crystal blue waters from which it came. Its peaceful gliding was effortless beauty, simply doing what it was designed to.

We were designed to abide. Previously, God had spoken to me in the midst of my striving saying, "You're doing a lot of doing, but not a whole lot of being." I was worn out trying to fix myself and frustrated, feeling like I was doing most of my "doing" out of obligation. There was no true satisfaction or sustainability in it. The Lord then took me through a process of understanding that when our "doing" comes from a place of obligation, insecurity, self-sufficiency, fear, or anything other than relationship with Him, it drains us. However, when we start to know God better, we can understand the kind of rest that comes with trusting Him. This rest is a state of the heart, a position of abiding in Him. Apart from Him, we really can't do anything worthwhile.[1]

That summer, I had been struggling to make time to pray and listen without any distractions. I felt guilty that I had gotten caught up in life and hadn't set aside my usual amount of time to stop and be quiet; but I'm so glad that God is patient with us. I don't believe He is exasperated by our humanity, frustrated and waiting for us to figure things out. He understands. He was never after our perfection; He is a Father pursuing His children. He just wanted *us*, wanted to build relationship with us through every step of the process (which is all of life). I think that's a big part of His plan for our lives anyway – the dreams, desires, and passions He put in our hearts to pursue – just creating opportunities for us to get close to Him. He loves to be a part of it all, and learning that simple truth brought me great liberation.

God's presence is not confined to a time of day or a specific environment. We don't have to do certain things to merit His love and affection or craft lengthy prayers with eloquent words to get His attention. His grace is sufficient, enough to carry us through each bend and turn on the path. In His love, there is no striving.

The change came when I stopped attempting to prove myself. I got to a place of recognizing that even though my plans and dreams for the future (or even just for today) are exciting and good, they actually mean nothing if I "get there" and don't know Jesus – really *know* Him. Because I can do good things for God, love people, read my Bible and pray, but if my relationship with Him isn't growing as a foundation for it all, it ends up being something I have manufactured (and those kinds of structures are never sturdy). It may look nice and put together on the outside, but what happens when the storm comes? As I have found in my own experience, it does not take long for these constructions to crumble if they are not laid upon One who is solid and steady, our Constant (see Psalm 127:1-2).

That day as I sat on the balcony, God reminded me that we begin to wither when we try to be our own source. We wind up back beneath the wreckage or trapped inside a cage with the door wide open. He just wants us to abide, to stay with Him. That's where the healing comes. That is where we discover true, lasting freedom. But isn't it so easy to get ahead of ourselves? With all the busyness of schedules and planning, self-sufficiency and quick fix remedies (or whatever it may be), if we're getting ahead of *ourselves,* where are we leaving God? I had to slow down and be still. Sometimes that's exactly what it takes to remind our souls that He is God and we are not (see Psalm 46).

As soon as I decided to let go, get quiet and refocus, everything changed. It doesn't matter so much what you *do.* If you focus on being with Him, He will tell you what to do when it's time to do something. When your eyes are fixed on Him, He will direct your vision with His own.

My experiences have led me to believe that the joy that comes from the moments of *being* with Jesus is far sweeter than any accomplishment; and when that is the case, it makes the accomplishments of life all the more satisfying because in the midst of success and overcoming, you can intimately know the heart of the One who longs to intimately bless yours. Such, I've found, is a life of divine purpose and fulfillment.

8
The Truth Gets In & The Truth Comes Out

Secrets often hold an illusionary power that makes us believe that by hiding and concealing, we can somehow maintain control over people and circumstances. However, contrary to what we've been taught and all we've observed in entertainment and media, keeping secrets is not glamorous and rarely gets us anywhere. It hardly supplies us with any real power. I think of it like the winding of a crank on a Jack-in-the-Box: all is well when the music is playing casually in the background of life, almost unnoticed. The puppet inside is kept hidden from those on the outside, seemingly just an ordinary box until one day it is wound so tightly that it suddenly pops open and everything that was unseen is out in the open.

In these moments of exposure we find that our God is the great Initiator. Although His motive is never to inflict pain on His own, He sometimes allows situations to progress to a point where the pressure causes us to crack, exposing what's going on inside.

He allows this because in all He does, He is eternally compelled by His love for us. Sometimes it takes getting to rock bottom to realize we've been standing on sand.

That's what happened to me one afternoon as I sat in my psychiatrist's office. At this point, I was being medicated for depression and generalized anxiety disorder, so I had to stop in every so often. My mom sat beside me and listened as I answered the doctor's questions for my check up. She asked how I was doing and if there was anything I wasn't telling her. I said no and tried to move things along so we could finish up and go. Right as we were about to leave, I looked to my right and noticed that my mom was crying. She wouldn't make eye contact with me. I had no idea why, but the doctor was just as curious and confused as I was. She asked my mom what was wrong and the answer came more blunt and brutal than I ever imagined it possibly could. The color left my face and was replaced with a cold panic as I heard my mom spill the truth that I was too afraid to admit myself: "I think she's making herself throw up."

I couldn't believe it. How did she know? The last set of reigns I held onto was ripped from my hands, my secret no longer hidden comfortably in the dark. My mask was torn off and all of my puppets were now out in the open. I sat there in my chair, horrified that I no longer had control. In fact, that was what I had been fighting for all along. The eating disorder, the anxiety, all of it – desperate attempts to be the one in charge, but that was never my right or my place. I had been resisting God and fighting for control for a long time and here was the height of the battle, fully realizing my defeat. All I could do now was surrender. That's what He had been waiting for the whole time, gently and lovingly winding me up so I could finally be securely unwound before Him. He doesn't cringe at our raw, open honesty. He sees it all anyway, whether we choose to bring it to Him or not. This was His original intent: for His children to be safely exposed in the comfort of His presence.

The very first word of identity God spoke over us was (and still is), "very good." After each bit of creation, God called it good. However, it wasn't until after he created mankind that He looked over all of it and declared that it was *very* good (Genesis 1:31). He finally rested in the completion of His work now that He had children who would reflect His image to the rest of creation. Keep in mind that this was before we were ever born or even a thought in our parents' minds, which means that God said we were very good before we ever did anything right or wrong, before we even had the chance to earn His approval or mess up trying. Why is it, then, that we so easily get caught beneath the measuring stick of the enemy? Who ever gave anyone – seen or unseen – the right to make us feel like we aren't good enough?

I'm sure it's safe to say that we have all felt this way at some point, but let me be the one to tell you that this standard does not exist. It is something that our world system, backed by the lies and schemes of a very real enemy, has convinced us is necessary to keep in mind at all times if we are ever going to be loved, successful, accepted – whatever it may be. This reaching and striving to be "good enough" has no point of arrival because the devil will never run out of lies. He will always tease and taunt us to exhaust us, discourage us, and steer us away from the confident hope we have in Jesus and our identity in Him (Ephesians 1:18-23).

If the devil can trick us out of our identity in Christ, then there's not much else he has to do to keep us from being effective in God's Kingdom; but if we really get ahold of the truth about who we are, then there is **nothing** satan can do to hold us back. If we believe that God is who He says He is, then we can also believe that we are who He says we are. We are His.

He is a good Father and He knows what He is doing. Like a parent who takes their child to the doctor to get shots, He stays close to our side, knowing that although it will be painful in the moment, it is ultimately for our benefit. We may not see all that it protects us from at the time, and we may never fully see, but we can trust His intentions and believe that His ways are higher.

It's a good thing my mom outed me that day. Shortly after, I started seeing a nutritionist to get treatment for the advanced stages of anorexia and bulimia. It helped to talk about my obsession with food and appearance, especially with someone who understood, but I was apathetic and unmotivated to change for several weeks. At the end of each visit, my nutritionist would give me simple homework assignments such as, "Eat a sandwich every day this week" or "get rid of the clothes you're holding onto for when you're 'thinner.'" For most, this would seem easy, but I was caught in an incredibly warped way of thinking. I was still dissatisfied with the way I looked and did not want to give up control or gain weight.

I did not know who I was. I didn't understand my worth or have any idea of the immensity of God's love for me, and I'm still learning. I was looking to others for approval and I was tangled up in the trap of comparison. My nutritionist addressed this issue once during one of our sessions. I was explaining to her why I thought I would feel more beautiful if I looked different and she said, "Hannah, you're comparing lions and giraffes."

She went on to explain the illustration like this: If a lion spends all of its time wishing it was as tall and thin as the giraffe, wishing it had spots like the giraffe and that it could reach the places high in the tree that the giraffe could, then the lion would miss out on all of its own potential. If the lion is constantly focused on what it is not, it doesn't realize all that it is and everything that it was specifically and purposefully created for. That's exactly what I was doing. I was a lion that didn't appreciate the value and strength of its own unique design.

When we put all our hope in something or someone else to validate us, we are never fully satisfied. I wanted to be loved and cherished and valued so badly that I thought, "If I look like her or do that better, then I will be loved. If I can just be with that person or achieve this goal, then people will be proud of me and I will be happy." I was searching for fulfillment in all the wrong places. I was searching for something that was already mine. I was trying to be something I already was.

God never wanted us to go through life feeling inadequate. That's why He sent Jesus to restore us to the identity we lost sight of along the way. In the beginning He deemed us worthy, and when the devil had convinced us otherwise, Jesus came to *re*-deem us. Now covered by the blood of Jesus, our Maker sees us flawless.

Since receiving salvation, I believed this in my head; but in my heart, I had still been acting out of a broken and corrupted belief system. I was covering up, hiding, and pretending most of the time. I was letting fear take the lead, even though I knew better.

Thinking back to Adam and Eve, this was very much their experience in the Garden. God created the man and woman naked. They were totally exposed in both the physical and spiritual sense. Nothing was hidden as they walked together daily and they were comfortable with God and each other. They had nothing else to compare it to. This was normalcy. This was God's design.

It wasn't until after they had second-guessed what God had said and fallen into satan's trap to sin that Adam and Eve felt shame and compelled to cover up and hide. The enemy's scheme is to make sin seem like not such a big deal, cheer us on through temptation until we give in, and then condemn us until we are miserably full of regret. He's like the big kid bully at school who pressures the younger kids to do something foolish, telling them it will be cool. Then he makes fun of them when they fall for it and goes to tell the teacher so *they* are the ones who get in trouble. He lures us in with reasonable-sounding almost-truths that tempt us into making decisions that temporarily satisfy our sinful nature; and then as soon as we give him what he wants, he piles on the guilt and shame.

Shame is one of the enemy's greatest tools in keeping us distant from God. In her book *Closer Than Your Skin: Unwrapping the Mystery of Intimacy with God,* Susan D. Hill writes, "In time, those trapped by shame speculate that God is not merely indifferent, but actually against them. They feel hopelessly flawed and irredeemable. Tragically, these beliefs are rarely spoken out loud, and therein lies their power."[1] The enemy will do whatever he can to keep us from believing the truth about who God is and who we are in relationship with Him. Satan will always be motivated by his hate for God's children because we are the ones who now possess all the riches of the Kingdom that he will never be able to gain for himself.

Not too long ago, I read a book called *Across All Worlds: Jesus Inside Our Darkness.*[2] In this book, C. Baxter Kruger explains the beauty of the Gospel in a way I had never seen it presented before. He talks about how the Good News is not only that Jesus came to take on every bit of our sin and die on our behalf so that we could be raised to new, eternal life with Him; but also that He came to live among us as one of us. He walked in our shoes, felt our pain, and experienced our struggles and temptations. He went through the process, and in every part He kept unbroken and uninterrupted intimacy with the Father through the Spirit. And now because we are seated with Christ and made right with God through His blood, we can experience that same fellowship and unbroken intimacy in the midst of our own processes.

The Gospel strips shame of its power because we are made new creations in Christ the moment we believe. The old has completely passed away and we are redefined in His love and made right with God, not by anything we have done or could ever possibly do, but purely by His grace (2 Corinthians 5:17;

Ephesians 2:1-10). And now we overcome not only by the blood of Jesus, but also by the word of our testimony (Revelation 12:10-11). We overcome by telling our stories. When we do, shame can no longer hold us, for its power is only valid in the unspoken corners of darkness.

When we speak up, shame's grip is lost; when we open up, Love can enter in and break off fear. Forever expelled from heaven and eternally in the absence of God's love, satan's only device is fear. Fear is the root of shame: the fear of being unacceptable in some way, the fear of being found out, the fear that what you have done (or what has been done to you) has left you beyond repair. But fear speaks only in lies. It is the truth that Love speaks that sets us free, even when it isn't easy to hear.

In a later visit to the nutritionist, I was confronted with reality. Though I had started to make an effort to get better and spent countless nights journaling my prayers and seeking the Lord's help, I was not aware of the gravity of what could happen if things didn't change. The tension in my mind was becoming unbearable and my strength was failing.

I sat down on the couch in my nutritionist's office, surrounded by fashionable throw pillows and inspirational quotes. She understood me, having been in the same position herself years prior to getting her degree so she could someday help girls like me who were still on the opposite side of overcoming. I usually felt better after leaving her office because she reminded me that I wasn't alone. She took the time to listen, but some days I didn't want to talk much.

One day she was asking me questions, trying to get me to open up about how I was feeling, but I wasn't giving her a whole lot to work with. I asked her something about how much longer she thought I would need treatment for, and I remember the way she replied, compassionate but almost begging me not to give up as she said, "Hannah, at this point, we're just trying to keep you alive."

I let out a breath I didn't realize I was holding and sat still with my limp arms across my lap and my head down, avoiding making eye contact with the truth. I felt like I should have been shocked, but I knew she wasn't lying. The doctors and counselors didn't want to scare me or my family, but things were not exactly looking up. In that moment I realized that I had a choice to make: I could either give up and settle back into hiding and defeat, or I could stand up, face the flaming arrows hurled in my direction, and get out of this pit.

Truth sets us free, not only when it takes root and residence in our hearts, but also when we are brave enough to let it out. When we keep our pain, fear, shame, unforgiveness, discouragement, and all the rest covered up inside, there is no healing or steps forward. Often times we stay stuck here, holding on to the brokenness we've become accustomed to, but when we are willing to be honest about where we are at and get it all out in the open, Jesus can come in and completely transform our hearts and minds.

I decided it was time for me to break free from the grip of shame and fear. I spoke up.

I need to stop these thoughts. I want a positive outlook on life. I want to know what it's like to go through one week where I don't have to worry. It's hard, this feeling is like being trapped. I want to get control of my emotions. I don't want to cry anymore. I want to let go of the pain and be strong. I want to be happy. I want to be someone people want to be around. I want to be a better friend, sister, daughter, girlfriend, and better person all together. I feel like if I don't change, I could lose all the people I love – something I can't stand to do. I need hope, and I'm starting to see it. I just have to grab onto it and not let go.

9
Opening Up: The Power of Words
& Our Stories

My heart used to be standing room only. People would pay a price to stay and never really get a chance to settle in because it was so crowded by the pain and fears I kept company with. It exhausted many and frustrated some, since they could never get a good view. They would leave dissatisfied and disappointed. As a result, I often felt more like a burden than anything else, but I was okay (and even comfortable) with the distance.

I am generally a quiet person, but for most of my childhood and adolescent years, I was paralyzed by fear and intimidation. I was too afraid to sing in front of people, too afraid to open up to people, too afraid to even share my thoughts and opinions. Fear kept me from embracing opportunities that came along the way. It kept me from enjoying school, relationships, and the thrill of taking risks. Fear kept me from moving forward and eventually introversion turned to isolation. After all this time I can still see how the years I spent afraid affected me.

I was absorbed with assumptions of what other people thought of me, constantly overthinking and overanalyzing each situation. So many times I held back for fear of what it might look like or sounds like on the outside, overly cautious of appearing foolish or doing anything that could lead to rejection. I had felt its sting just enough to turn my heart callous and I gradually began denying people access until walls surrounded the premises. I was deceived, thinking that this was safety when it was only strongholds. They were walls that kept me trapped inside my bondage.

Suppressing my emotions became a coping mechanism that trained my heart to push aside the pain so I never had to deal with it. I ignored the root issues, so they grew into twisted branches that dug deeper and deeper, making them harder to remove with each new offense taken.

Sometimes my friends would come to me for advice or prayer and I would take the time to listen and encourage them where I could. I made sure to be available to them night and day, sometimes stretching myself a little too thin in order to honor an internal vow I had made in my own defense: to never let anyone else feel as alone as I had in my own pain. If it were up to me, no one would have ever gone a day thinking their pain was insignificant, believing that no one cared or understood. More than anything, I wanted people to feel safe to open up to me and know that I would never judge them. I wanted to love people like Jesus does and I still feel this way, but back then these passions were misdirected and motivated by prideful justifications of my own wounds. I would end these conversations with a smile and walk away in the company of my own bitter unforgiveness and sorrow.

I wanted so badly to be let into the hearts of others, but I felt like such a hypocrite when I lay in bed at night realizing that I was the worst example of vulnerability for them to follow. How could I possibly expect others to want to confide in a girl who had kind words to offer, but kept them at arm's length? As much as I longed to feel seen and understood, my heart had learned to react in fear when people got too close, so it would never be long before it turned and ran. Surely we are all after a greater substance of connection and hope.

I wanted that connection. I wanted to be brave enough to open up and let people see what was in my heart. I wanted to be like Jesus and share the hope He had given me with the people around me, but how could they see it if I was always hiding? I didn't want to hide anymore, but for a while I was frustrated with myself. Why was I still dealing with all this stuff? I had prayed plenty of times and asked God to take it away and heal me. I didn't understand why as soon as I stopped cutting and the depression got better, I was dying physically due to the effects of the eating disorder. I decided I wanted to live and then my body wasn't giving me the option.

Once again I was faced with a choice: either give in to the lies and attacks the enemy was trying to drown me in, or hold on to the truth of God's Word, however invisible and impossible that hoping seemed at the time.

I spent many nights alone in my room listening to worship music and waiting for something to happen. I journaled prayers until my hand could hardly grip the pen and poured my heart out, asking God to break me open if that's what had to be done in order for me to be whole. I wanted to believe the truth that was starting to sink in as I read my Bible and asked the Holy Spirit to renew my mind. I was desperate for hope and I knew I couldn't find it anywhere else. I had gone long enough trying to fix my problems with Band-Aids. It was time to face the truth, my pain, and myself.

I finally realized how ineffective my hiding was all along. God saw all my pain. In fact, He knew it better than I did. From the beginning He has known my thoughts, and as a result He understands exactly why I do the things I do and why I feel the things that stir in my heart. He gets it (Psalm 33:13-15). He fully sees and fully knows His children. To me, that was a revelation that brought relief and opened the door to a surrender that, although risky, was more secure than any stronghold I'd ever found comfort in.

Over time this transformation took place, but it was not a quick process. It started with the way I talk. For years, I let the negativity that was in my head sink into my heart and it came out through my mouth, because what we say overflows from our hearts (Luke 6:45). One time I asked the Lord to teach me how to guard my heart and He showed me that in order to guard your heart, you have to guard your mind. Our minds are like a garden. God, satan, and the world around us are all planting seeds; but as with any garden, what you tend to grows.

The things we think about and dwell upon become what make up the root system of our believing. As we pay attention to a thought – whether good or bad – it's like we are watering the seed and giving it space to break open and expand, stretching its roots deep down where they take up residence in our hearts. When these roots are truth, the result is a secure foundation of love that we can stand on and an anchor of hope for our souls; when they are lies, the result is fear, bondage, and skewed perceptions of God, people, and ourselves.

A mentor once taught me that thoughts turn into feelings, feelings turn into desires, and desires shape our behavior (our speech and actions). This is why it is imperative to take our thoughts captive when they are just thoughts and nothing more (2 Corinthians 10:3-5). Basically, this means that we have to put them in their place. But when something is taken out, we have to be intentional about filling the void with truth. Otherwise another lie will try to squeeze its way in. For me this meant getting rid of negativity and replacing it with God's Word, which is life and hope, and it never returns void (Isaiah 55:11). For example, if I started to feel anxious, I would say out loud, "He has not given me a spirit of fear, but of power, love, and a sound mind (2 Timothy 1:7)." I would remind myself that He knows the plans He has for me, that He never leaves or forsakes me, He works all things together for my good, and absolutely nothing in all creation can ever separate me from His love.

Eventually, that became my default instead of worrying about the future and other things that are out of my control. This is an ongoing process and I still have to consciously choose truth every day, but it gets easier the more you surrender yourself to the Lord and ask for the Holy Spirit's help. As I grew in the truth and God started tearing down my walls, I stepped into greater levels of freedom.

Another bit of beneficial knowledge I gained along the way was the awareness of the weight our words carry. When I was a student at Christ for the Nations Institute, I had the opportunity to take a class on spiritual warfare. When discussing this topic, my teacher brought up Deuteronomy 19:15, which talks about how nothing can be established as truth unless there are two or three witnesses. Because ours is a triune God (Father, Son, and Holy Spirit), He already has three witnesses and doesn't even need our agreement in order to be truth. However, our accuser satan is only one witness. But when we take the bait and give in to his lies, we become the second witness and his lies become reality to us.

Thankfully, our gracious God has given us His Spirit whose job is to lead us into all truth and be our helper. He has made Himself completely available to us at all times, and as we submit ourselves to His will and leadership, He is faithful to show us the areas in our mindsets where we need some realignment.

114

Sometimes it's easy to get caught up in discouragement when we don't see the change happening right away, but thinking back to the garden illustration, growth always starts with the roots. It takes time for the roots to grow, but if we are faithful even when we can't see anything above the surface, we will eventually see the fruit of what we have committed to in the process.

Over the course of a few months, I began to see a shift in my perspective as I read my Bible and prayed. Each day I would say to the Lord in total honesty, "I don't want to, but I *want* to want to, so please help me believe and trust you." (I still pray this all the time.) Soon I felt faith rising in me and I became more confident than I ever had been – all from stepping back, surrendering my weakness in exchange for His strength, and letting the Holy Spirit lead my steps.

God had taught me so much through my own struggles and I wanted to share it with other people. I decided it was time, so I approached my youth pastor and asked if I could speak in chapel at school one Wednesday. I shared some of my story with him and explained why I wanted to tell it to the rest of the students. I was afraid, but God had put it on my heart, so I decided to take the risk of being vulnerable in front of my peers and go for it.

I carefully prepared my notes and practiced over and over in my room, asking God to give me the words to say. I felt like I was supposed to talk about my scars. For a long time, I was ashamed of them and I wore long sleeves all year round – even in Texas summer – to keep them out of sight. I had stopped cutting, but I was embarrassed to look down and see the marks that had represented failure and pain to me. I remember the way God helped me see differently while I was reading in the book of Galatians one day. When I got to verse 17 of chapter 6, I soaked in the truth that forever changed my perspective: "From now on, don't let anyone trouble me with these things. For I bear on my body the scars that show I belong to Jesus. (NLT)" It was no longer a failure or handicap; it was my testimony. I had overcome, and now my scars were a picture of redemption and healing.

I started jotting down some notes about scars that came to mind. Scars are marks that represent a wound that has healed, but not exactly to way it was before. They might not always be physical, but in our hearts we all have scars that represent stories of brokenness and pain. I was comforted as I read and understood that now I can use my story as a beacon of light in the darkness to help others overcome. And as if that wasn't exciting enough, I heard Jesus' tender whisper echo in my heart, "I have scars too." No longer would I feel disqualified or beyond repair. He had traded my ashes for beauty and gave me a story to tell.

The first time I told my story, it surprised me as much as it did those who heard it. So many people came up to me afterward and said that they had no idea I was dealing with all that. Several other people came to me confessing that they also battled depression and struggled with cutting, and I got to walk with them through their own healing and encourage them in their process. If I had never spoken up, I wonder how many of those people would have still felt alone and stayed in hiding.

Telling my story that day sparked something in me that broke off the power of shame and began the unwinding of fear's grip on me. I was no longer intimidated by my weakness, but glad that God's strength and glory could shine through it.

10
This is Not What I Expected

I remember being a senior in high school and thinking I had it all figured out. I had my list of dreams and a whole lot of ambition, and I was ready go after the perfect plan I'd mapped out for my life. I was going to get my degree and run with it, which would have been fine I'm sure, but that was *my* plan. And I'm sure we have all experienced to some extent what happens when we tell God, "Not my will but yours be done." It's funny; He actually takes our prayers seriously.

A few months before I graduated, I was doing really well. I felt pretty steady emotionally, and although I was in a lot of physical pain, I was choosing to trust the Lord. I had peace from His Word and His Spirit that despite what doctors said and the diagnoses I received, everything would be okay.

I had looked into a couple different universities and filled out a few applications, but nothing was set in stone yet. I had ideas about where I wanted to go and what I wanted to do, but nothing fell into place or felt quite like I had hoped it would. During that time, my friend Puckett was attending a Bible school called Christ for the Nations Institute (CFNI) in Dallas, which wasn't too far from where I lived. He was in the Worship and Technical Arts major, and he would tell me all about the things he was learning in school. I was intrigued. I had never considered Bible school, but he told me I should come visit sometime and sit in on some of his classes. I thought about it, and the more I did, the more I wanted to go see what it was all about.

I remember going to one of their weekly Tuesday night services and being completely in awe. There is nothing like standing in a room full of people worshiping God together. Soon after that, I came to visit Puckett in class. I sat on the edge of my seat listening to the teachers talk about facets of God and worship I had never even considered before. I remember feeling right at home there. It wasn't long before I sent in my application. I was accepted and began packing up my things to prepare for this new adventure. Though I never would have chosen this path for myself, I had peace knowing God had orchestrated it and it was much better than anything I could have dreamed of on my own.

August came and I said goodbye to everything that was familiar. I moved in as early as I could so I would have some time to settle in and adjust, but when I got to CFNI, I felt so small. There were hundreds of people from all over the world, all different ages, with all different languages, passions, and stories. It was overwhelming and amazing. I had never experienced anything like it. It was the farthest I had ever ventured out of my comfort zone, but even though it was scary, I knew that's where the growth would happen if I let it.

Puckett had graduated the semester before I came, but my good friend Brandon started at the same time as me, and I figured having him there would help me make friends. For twelve years, I had been at the same school with the same people and now I was going from a class of twenty to one in the upper hundreds. I had never really needed to go out of my way to make friends growing up, since I had met most of my classmates in elementary school and went to church with several of them. Everything about this next step was new and I was intimidated to say the least, but it was exciting nonetheless.

I slowly started getting to know my roommates, but they were a few semesters ahead of me, so I still didn't really know anyone in my class. After orientation one day, I was standing in line for lunch when the girl in front of me turned around and introduced herself to me. She started asking me questions and at first I felt so awkward and uncomfortable, not knowing what to say or how to carry a conversation, but despite my short answers she continued talking to me. We ended up eating lunch together with Brandon and some of the people he had met, and we really hit it off. Megan and I were fast friends and stuck together all year long.

Shortly after the semester began I went through a difficult time of letting go. I had built up plans in my heart again and because I had put all my hopes and expectations in them, I was devastated when they fell through. When I no longer had control over the situation, God was finally able to come in and say, "Hey, I'm right here with you. Are you still in this with me?" Each time I would say yes, hoping that at some point my motives and desires would change to match the commitment I so desperately wanted to make to Him wholeheartedly.

I remember being in the upstairs balcony one morning during chapel when I felt the Lord ask me, "How much are you willing to give me?" I replied, "Everything, Lord. Of course, you can have it all." (Who is going to deny Jesus after all He has done and continues to do for us, right?) But He said, "I'll ask you again when you can say that and mean it." I was a little shocked, and offended even, thinking surely He knows I meant it; but the more I thought about it, the more I realized just how much I was actually holding onto. In several areas, I had put my own comfort and convenience above what I knew God was asking me and leading me to do. Something had to change.

Since I have wrestled with fear for so long, I don't think it's any coincidence that the first part of my healing was a journey learning about the remedy: love. I started to open up to Megan about how broken I was feeling, how scared I was to let go and surrender everything to God, and how painful I knew it would be (even though I knew it was the right – and best – thing to do). She was patient with me and took the time to walk with me through all of it. I was very thankful for the gift of our friendship and how thoughtful God was to give me someone to help me along the way.

After a long day of feeling overwhelmed, I finally hit my breaking point a few weeks into this healing process. As I'm sure all of us have discovered in some form, when you hit the breaking point, everything that was carefully suppressed inside spills out (and I think that's exactly where He wants us for these sorts of situations, no more hiding or faking it). I was sitting in my car one evening pouring out my heart to God and being honest with Him about how frustrated and offended and hurt I felt. I felt forgotten and rejected, insignificant and hopeless – anything but loved.

When He spoke, I didn't expect what I heard: "I want you to learn how to love others *first*, before you receive it." My initial reaction was to make a list of reasons why this wasn't fair because I didn't deserve to be treated this way, but God opened my eyes to see things in a completely different light, showing me that everyone is deserving of love, no matter what. It doesn't matter if they return it or appreciate it, or if they even care – everyone is worthy of being loved. So I embarked on a journey of loving people God's way.

I told Megan about it and asked if she wanted to join me, that way I would have some accountability and we could encourage each other when it got hard. She quickly agreed, and for the next thirteen weeks we practiced loving. We went through 1 Corinthians 13:4-7 and took on one of the attributes of love each week. The first week was challenging, right off the bat: patience. After the first day alone, I was so glad I had asked Megan to do it with me. It was so helpful having someone to study Bible verses about love with and discuss what we were learning. That made it much easier to stick it out the remaining weeks.

We made up challenges for each other based on people and situations we were dealing with at the time, and we prayed for God to give us opportunities and help us be patient when they came. The next week, we practiced being kind, and so on all the way down the list. By the time we got to the end, I could hardly recognize the person I was at the beginning anymore. The transformation in my heart was undeniable. I never anticipated such a tremendous shift to occur when I simply started focusing on others more, but God knows what He's doing and the change in me was proof.

When learning to love people well, with honesty and intention, it is inevitable that you will run into challenges and have to confront your "self" in the process. Sometimes it's a hard pill to swallow. There is no more reacting in anger, trying to justify yourself or making passive remarks, because love keeps no record of wrongs. No more holding onto offenses, because love surrenders its rights to judgment and bitterness and trades them for forgiveness. On days when you want to quit because the journey is exhausting, it's a humbling reality check to be reminded that love never gives up or loses hope. It endures all things.

In moments of frustration, I had to face what was really in my heart. It wasn't always an easy thing to see, but because God was the one unraveling me and teaching me, holding my hand the whole way, I could face myself, let go of disappointments, and then embrace the beauty of who I was becoming. And who I am still in the process of becoming today.

A year later, I was in Ireland going back over everything I had learned so I could share it with a church there in Belfast. I asked God what I could say that would be beneficial and encouraging to them, trying to figure out how I could possibly condense it all. I went back to 1 Corinthians 13 and tried to find some direction. When I got to the end of the passage, the very last verse caught my attention: "Three things will last forever – faith, hope, and love – and the greatest of these is love."

When I finished reading, I wondered why love is the greatest. It wasn't that I disagreed, but I was curious because faith and hope are pretty vital too. Then 1 John 4:8 came to mind, where it says that God Himself is love, and it clicked. Because of God – because He is Love – that's the only reason we are able to have faith and hope. Then the gears really started turning. I went back to the beginning of 1 Corinthians 13 and read it differently: God is patient and kind. God doesn't keep a record of our wrongs. God is jealous for us because of His love for us, but He is not selfish. He is incarnate love in the person of Jesus, and when we practice loving, we are practicing becoming more like Him.

I could hardly believe it. No wonder I was seeing things so differently. I wasn't just learning about love, I was getting to know Jesus, and my developing relationship with Him was what was transforming my entire life. Love was casting out my fear, just like I had heard it would all along; except "it" was a He.

The more I got to know Jesus, the more I got to see glimpses of His heart. I found that His heart is to serve, to give, and to never hold back out of greed or fear. It's to honor others and treat everyone with respect, regardless of what you think you deserve in return. His heart is to be patient with people in their process, not getting upset when they don't get it the first time. Little by little, my motives slowly started lining up with His. The desires of His heart were changing mine.[1]

When I started to understand His heart more clearly (why He does what He does and why He tells us to do certain things), it became easier for me to trust Him and believe that He really *is* who He says He is and He really *will* do what He says He will do. I'll be honest, I still have moments of doubt. I still have days when I'm not convinced of His goodness in my circumstances, but now those feelings of worry, fear, confusion, or apathy serve as indicators that I need to redirect my focus back to Him.

I am thankful to have had the opportunity to be surrounded by godly friends and teachers at CFNI while I was going through these transitions and "growth spurts." It really made a difference to be in an atmosphere of faith, surrounded by others who were experiencing miracles, big and small, in their own lives almost every day (which is God's design for the Church anyway). It encouraged me to hear the testimonies of healing and provision and overcoming, and it made me even more excited to realize that God's presence is just as powerful outside of CFNI. Those kinds of encounters and transformations can take place anywhere at anytime.

One day it happened to me in my dorm room. It was time to take my depression and anxiety medications again, so I walked over to my dresser and pulled open the drawer to take them out. I picked up two small, orange prescription bottles and shook them around in my hand. I pressed down on the cap so I could twist one of them open. Looking down into the tube filled with tiny pills, I wondered if I'd still be looking at the same scene years down the road. I certainly hoped not. I twisted the lid back on, set the bottles on top of my dresser, and stood in silence for a moment.

Over the past few days, I had considered what it might be like to stop taking my medicine. I was feeling really good, and I had heard so many stories of other people being healed of depression and anxiety. I decided, why not? If God could do it for them, He could do it for me. I picked up the bottles and walked into the bathroom. Without even really thinking it through, I twisted both of them open and flushed all their contents away. There was no turning back now.

The next day, doubt began to cast its shadow as I woke up hoping I had done the right thing. Was I going to find myself in the same mess I'd been in before and end up having to get new prescriptions since I had thrown all of mine away? What had I gotten myself into? Yesterday it all seemed so simple.

I got up and started my day. I went to chapel and then to class, and I felt fine. In bed that night, I wondered if it was just a lucky day with fun things to distract me and no triggers set off that would send me into a panic. The next day came and went, and then the next day, until a month had gone by and nothing happened.

It felt too good to be true. What was the catch? Where was the sudden snap that would spiral my emotions out of control and back into depression? It never came. Sure, there were hard days and things that made me upset, but from then on I never got stuck in the pit of depression or anxiety again. I don't believe I'll ever have to go back.[2]

I'm done believing that healing is only for some people in some circumstances. It doesn't always make sense, and I will never be able to fully understand why we don't get to see the healing on this side of heaven sometimes, but I still believe in healing because I believe in Jesus. I've experienced Him as Healer, and now I know it's true.

Now my beliefs center on the fact that Jesus is enough, without having to analyze all the "whys". His blood was enough to save me before I even met the criteria to be a disciple. His love was enough to change me before I ever backed away into hiding and blocked Him out, because He never stopped pursuing me. He is still pursuing me, and His active presence in my life is enough to heal and restore me day by day as I continue walking with Him, even when I don't understand or I don't see the results of my obedience right away. Everything He does is right and perfect, and if we say yes to Him, we will never miss it. We will never miss out. This is the freedom He has made available to us who are His own.

11
The Contagious Healing /
Stay Your Course

I found myself in my psychiatrist's office again for another routine checkup. It had been about a month since I stopped taking my medications and I was really looking forward to telling her about how much better I was doing without them. God had done a miraculous thing for me when I stepped out in faith and I was excited to tell people about it whenever I got the chance.

People who had known me before were shocked when they saw how different I was. The change that took place in my heart overflowed into every area of my life: how I talked, how I listened to others, how I carried myself. Whenever I came home from school to visit with friends, several of them commented on the "glow" I had. They noticed something different about me, so I expected my doctor to have the same reaction.

She came into the room and sat down at her desk across from my mom and me. She started asking how I was doing, how school was going, and if

I was still taking my prescriptions. When I happily told her no, she gave me a stern look of disapproval. I tried to explain that I was feeling much better; that I had felt fine since the day I stopped taking them. In fact, I had been feeling much better than I ever did when I was on them. She looked very upset with me, so I didn't say anything else. She took a deep breath and looked me in the eye as she explained that no one should ever quit taking those medications without consulting a doctor first.

Apparently it was very dangerous to stop taking them the way I did, because my brain had become used to – and even dependent upon – certain chemicals in the pills she had prescribed. For this reason, my brain could have gone into shock and my body might not have responded well at all. Although it was surreal listening to everything she was saying and trying to take it all in, I left that doctor's office for the very last time that day knowing that without a doubt, God had healed me.

My mom was just as surprised as I was. She saw the transformation in me and knew I was telling the truth. She had been there for the entire process.

At the time, my mom was suffering from rheumatoid arthritis. Constantly in pain, she was desperate for relief. After we left the doctor that day, she and I talked about God's healing power and how it's the same today as it was in the stories from the Bible. My mom prayed and decided she was going to step out in faith too. She hasn't taken any of her medication since.

It didn't stop there. Once my mom and I had both experienced healing, she began believing like she never had before. During that same time, my sister was taking medicine for ADHD that made her act strange and lose her appetite. She wasn't herself when she took it and my mom didn't want to see her child dependent on a medication that made her feel that way. Not long after, Kuri was off of her medication too.

Sometimes when my mom and I talk about our healing, people say it was probably only a mental thing or that Kuri just "grew out of her ADHD." Not everyone agrees and many try to justify circumstances like these with logic, but that's okay. It's not worth arguing about. We have seen and know the work God has done, and that's enough. I am not an expert on healing by any means, but I believe in it. I believe that the same blood that was able to save us is able to sustain us; able to heal us completely, simply because that's what the truth of the Bible declares over those who are in Christ.[1]

The healing process isn't the same for everyone. I believe that God can heal in a moment, but sometimes we don't see the change right away. Sometimes the physical transformation is instantaneous, sometimes it is gradual, and sometimes we don't get to see it in our lifetime at all; but God knows which method is best for where we're at, what will best accomplish His will: to teach us, heal us, grow us, and be glorified through us as a testimony to the world around us.

There is a story in John[2] about a man who comes to Jesus begging him to heal his son who was about to die. He was desperate and knew something had to be done as soon as possible. Maybe he had gone to every doctor, tried every remedy, and even had the religious leaders pray for his son, and still nothing had changed. I imagine it must have been heart wrenching for him to watch his son suffer. He must have been scared, waking up each day wondering if it would be the last to spend with him, if he would have to bury his own child. I'm sure it felt risky for him to go searching for Jesus, because what if he didn't get there in time? What if his son died when he was still traveling and he didn't get to say goodbye? What if Jesus refused to come back with him? What if Jesus couldn't do anything to help? What if he didn't have time?

This father did not let the "what ifs" of fear and worry keep him from stepping out in faith. He knew that regardless of the outcome, the journey was worth it. It had to be. If anyone had the ability change their situation, Jesus did. He had nothing to lose, so he came boldly. Upon arrival, Jesus made a statement about the doubt that so many people in the towns had settled into. Many wanted Jesus to prove himself. They had the "I'll believe it when I see it" attitude, but Jesus was trying to get them to see that that's not the point.

The whole idea of faith is making a choice to believe *before* our eyes ever get a chance to be convinced or swayed in any direction. Faith is confident hoping, a trust in God that is not based on any physical evidence for or against our case. The faith Jesus is looking for is hearts willing to take the leap before even looking over the edge of the cliff to see how far the drop is. This kind of faith doesn't calculate the distance or the danger; it just believes that whether the landing is rocky or smooth, God will see them through.

This man probably heard what Jesus said and perhaps he wondered if he had the faith Jesus required. In that moment, he was likely tempted to back out. He could have let intimidation take the reigns, and turned around to head home discouraged and defeated; but he gave the devil no foothold, no room to talk him out of it. I picture him approaching Jesus: the look of pain and determination in his eyes, likely dark and swollen from tears or exhaustion from the sleepless nights he spent aching for his helpless, dying child.

I see a father who had run out of options walking up to the One who had the power to wipe out death and all of its affiliates. This man may have felt undeserving, unqualified, unlikely, and unsure, but with every ounce of strength and composure he could muster, he now stood face to face with Jesus and pleaded on behalf of the son he could not stand to lose. I can hear the urgency in his voice as he tried to explain the situation and stress the time to Jesus. It was running short and he needed God now more than ever. "Please come now."

Jesus looked at the man and really saw him. He saw this father who had come a long way for his son. He saw the love that had motivated the journey and the risk involved, sacrificing moments with his precious son who might not be conscious for much longer to inquire about healing from a man people said was the Son of God. I'm sure the father was trying to hold it together, face to face with his only hope, but Jesus knew the deep sorrow inside of him because Jesus saw his heart.

Our Jesus considers us in the light of the Father's great love for us, taking account of our suffering with compassion. When he hears our requests, He remembers our pain as He felt it on the cross when He took it all upon himself. But it is not our pain that moves Him; it is our faith.

Jesus' response to the father was to send him home because his son was going to live. The man believed Him and started his journey home. At this point, the man had seen no change. He didn't know how his son was doing or if there was any improvement at all, he just had to wait and hope and continue walking. What if he had stayed there in the city and tried to convince Jesus to come back with him because he couldn't just take His word for it? What if he had given in to fear and hopelessness and refused to return home because he wanted to avoid the expected announcement of his son's death? If he had stayed there, he would have missed something miraculous.

While he was still on his way, he ran into some of his servants who were coming to find him. Hardly able to contain their excitement, they raced to tell him the news: His son was well! Now the father still hadn't seen with his own eyes yet, but because of his faith that moved him to act on what Jesus had said, this report brought him great relief and peace. Because he had taken hold of the assurance that came with Jesus' command, the father was able to continue believing for the rest of the journey until his eyes finally confirmed what his faith was promised.

As the father talked with his servants on their way back, they discussed the details of everything that had just happened. He asked them when his son started to feel better, and when they told him the time, the father was shocked. His son was healed the exact moment Jesus spoke the words. It's no wonder why when they returned and told the story to everyone else, their entire household was saved.

Often times we believe for healing and then grow weary on the journey back; but when Jesus speaks the word, it is done. We may not see it or even come across any evidence of change until much further along in the process, but if we stay in the same place, we might just miss out on a moment of divine intervention that will encourage and fuel our faith for the rest of the journey.

Our processes are all different and unique for a reason. Through our trials and overcoming, God gives us something – or rather, draws something out of us – to share with the world during the specific part of creation's timeline that He has placed us in and trusted us with. Our obedience can end up leading our entire household (or sphere of influence) to faith in our healing God.

Do not settle into doubt on the journey back. His word is enough to sustain us the whole way until our eyes finally confirm the promise of our faith.

12
One Step at a Time / We Need Each Other

My friend John once said that time is a pretty good storyteller. I have found this to be true in my own process, especially when it comes to trusting God. So many times I have found myself discontent and frustrated because I wasn't where I wanted to be in life and things weren't falling into place the way I thought they would. To be honest, in those moments I did not appreciate the season of life I was in or what God was doing at that time. I didn't trust Him with the steps. I wanted to have it all figured out already, but my impatience hindered me from seeing the goodness God was displaying all around me right where I was.

When I think of the growth process, I tend to look at plants for a visual. Take a flower, for instance: You can't tell a seed to hurry up. Try as you may and be as forceful as you'd like, but rushing will not change the fact that a seed needs time to take root so that it can build up the strength necessary to support the weight of what it will soon carry above the surface. If a flower didn't have a chance to grow its roots, it wouldn't be able to hold the flower sturdy and provide the nutrients it needed in order to stay healthy and continue growing.

The same is true of us. We can't rush through the process because if we hurry things along and refuse to commit to being present with the Lord, we miss out on some major root work. When we fail to appreciate the beauty in the moments, we miss out on the wonder that is found in the details. We aren't able to soak up the fullness of His truth, which works like fertilizer. Instead, we settle for sand and build on a foundation that will just as quickly crumble beneath us when the storms come.

Sometimes it takes a while to see the change that's happening in our hearts, but that doesn't mean it isn't happening. A lot of the time it happens in ways we wouldn't expect, like when a flower starts to poke its way through the soil. It doesn't come up fully bloomed and brilliant with color. In fact, there are times during this stage when the flower can even be mistaken for a weed. Many people stop here. They see the beginning of what has been developing inside of them coming to the surface and they are confused or displeased because it wasn't what they were hoping for right away. But we can't stop here. This is only the push before the breakthrough.

When we choose to hold on even when we can't see, we get to enjoy the beauty of the final result, resting in the confidence that what we've built will stand because we know the intricacies of its structure and the intention of its design. These are the things God reveals to us in the "meantime." It doesn't always make sense, but God sees the end from the beginning, so we can trust Him.

For a long time, I couldn't get the trust thing down. (It's still a work in progress, but I think it's meant to be that way for all of life, growing in faith throughout the process until we are finally standing before Him completely undone.) I used to worry constantly about whether I was getting it right. Is this the right relationship? Is this the right job? Am I where I'm supposed to be? Was that the right thing to say? And so on. I would often find myself frustrated, confused, weighed down by all my anxiety, and feeling absolutely helpless. It was very distracting and it took away from the enjoyment of where I was. I didn't understand that if I just trust God to lead me in the steps, I wouldn't ever miss what He has for me. Worrying about what's going to happen next never changed the fact that it will happen the same way it would if I hadn't wasted so much time worrying about it; because in fact, worry is a result of misplaced trust. We just have to take it one step at a time.

Steps are defined as, "a measure or action, especially one of a series taken in order to deal with or achieve a particular thing."[1] Not only does our Jesus know the plan, the process, and the end from the beginning; He knows every step. He knows where we're going and every single movement that will get us there. He directs us not only in which path to take, but carefully shows us where to place our foot as we land the next step. Of course, this includes the steps that wind up in an uncomfortable spot or a place where we might have to reach a little further. He knows that, and He's aware that we often do not enjoy those steps. However, He designed your path very specifically in order to strengthen you the way

146

you need to be strengthened so that when you reach certain places in your journey, you will possess the skills needed to continue on with hope and resolve; because you will have seen Him come through for you, molding a faith in His unchanging nature that you can cling to when things are looking grim. Even if the next step doesn't look promising, He's right there holding onto you.

Sometimes trust is much easier said than done. Although God makes His way plain to us by seeking Him and through His Word, in our humanness we tend to overcomplicate that which was meant to be simple and childlike. There's that whole head-to-heart transition where we often struggle to get past blockage we've allowed to be glazed over with time, passages clogged with the gradual build-up of avoided confrontation of issues. It's never fun to face our pain, but in my experience I have found that the pain of pressing through and holding on for healing is much better than the ache of unresolved hurt festering inside.

We typically judge our present by our past and the pain we hold onto usually filters our perspectives. It's the natural thing to do, to learn to perceive life based on personal experience. However, I think we got a bit off course along the way. The enemy is tricky. He has a system that simultaneously tempts us to disconnect from our past entirely and also remain a slave to it. At times, one may sound more appealing than the other, but he baits us with both and most of the time we don't even realize he's done it until we feel the aftermath stirring inside us with regret: the exhaustion of running as fast and as far as you can to reach freedom (that's actually just on the other side of surrender to God), or the discontentment of settling into the comfort and supposed safety of complacency.

After years of falling for the devil's trap, I finally realized that we were meant to embrace the past. When we are able to accept and work through the things that we have done and that have been done to us, there is relief. There is rest in the safety of surrender to our loving God and Father. When we release the past to Him to be used for our good and His glory, the exchange is grace that enables us to understand the significance of all our yesterdays, todays, and tomorrows.

Although the pain we experience in relation to others can leave us hesitant to trust anymore, it is possible to break down the walls and open up again. When we are willing to be vulnerable and take the risk of exposure that comes with relationship, there is beauty in the outcome. And when we are open, togetherness is the result. Unity comes without us striving for it, which was God's design for His people from the start. There should be no competing or comparison in the Body, only functioning in love and peace the way it was meant to function, because when a body functions in the proper way, it is healthy and able to do all that it was created for.

The enemy wants us to think that shrinking away and closing up will lead to safety (and for a little while it may seem like it does), but those kinds of strongholds are nothing but false security. They are counterfeits of our true Stronghold, which is Christ.[2] If the devil can convince you that you're alone, or that you're the only one going through what you're going through, then he's got you. When he tricks us into isolation, we are starved of the togetherness we need in order to function properly and we begin to deteriorate from the inside out.

The truth is, we are not alone. And the truth is, we can't do it alone. We need each other and we need each other's stories. I strongly believe that the will of God for our lives involves relationships. It isn't complete without it. It's like living a healthy lifestyle: you can eat right and drink lots of water, and even run and do some pushups or lunges here and there, but you can only get so strong without lifting weights.

In my experience I've found that if you're going after the dreams God put in your heart, serving and doing good things even, but you're doing it alone or somehow become "too busy" to invest in relationships, you're missing it. I truly don't think that God's plan is ever solely dependent on us and what we do. We need Him and we also need the people He has put around us.

It's easy to quickly forget that part and become oblivious to the detail involved in His orchestration of where we are and the others who are in the same seasons of life in the same span of time. I don't think it's any coincidence. Think about it: God planned for you to be alive right now because He knew that there would be other people living right now who need to hear your story. You have something so unique to offer the world, something that no one else could ever contribute to the people that you could contribute to. And God has divinely appointed people in your own life to do the same for you.

If you really want to get strong and build up your muscles – even if only for better stability and protective purposes – you have to lift weights. It hurts sometimes. It leaves you sore and tired, and you may even want to quit some days, but the results are proof that the effort pays off. It just requires intentionality on our part. The same is true in relationships. We need that "iron sharpening iron" dynamic at work in our lives as we are ever becoming more like Jesus.

Of course, it's never easy starting out. If you aren't used to going to the gym regularly, it can be a challenge to get up and go, making it a priority in your routine. But the more you do it, the more you want to do it because you start feeling the change and seeing your progress, even when it hurts. When you decide to hang in there and make time for relationships, you will see yourself gradually getting stronger, able to take on more. You will feel better, even on the hard days, knowing that you have people standing firm with you in the fight. You will be more defined because if it's the right relationships, they will speak truth into your life, reminding you who you are and encouraging you no matter what part of your story you're in.

I think we should start being brave and letting people in again, especially in the Church. I think we need to start being humble enough to admit we can't do what God has called us to do on our own.

Maybe you've been hurt in relationships, maybe even in the Church. I know what that's like. It's painful and it's real, but the enemy loves to exaggerate our hurt and use it to lure us into bitterness and isolation if we aren't careful. I know the pain of rejection, inconsistency, and people not following through. I've been on both the giving and receiving side of that pain. But the thing is, we cannot do Christianity like working in an office building where we're all going to the same place, but doing our own work in our own cubicles with walls dividing us. I believe we were made to live in complete togetherness as a healthy Body.

For me, it has been a process of reaching out and also allowing others to reach out to me. It was and continues to be a process of forgiving and being forgiven, showing grace and receiving grace. I used to resist and shut down any affection, invitation, or even encouragement from others. In my pride I thought I knew what was best for me and that I didn't need other people's input, but in reality all that ever did was keep me exactly where I was. When I refused to let others be involved in my life, I wasn't growing near as much as I could have been if I had let them in. Over time, I started to realize this and I asked the Lord to humble my stubborn, prideful, calloused heart. When my requests began to line up with God's will and desires for my life, things started to change, and my selfishness began to fade and be replaced with the desire to love others well. My wants became less about me and more about how I could honor God and represent Him the right way, especially in relationships.

My heart slowly started to open up again and I began to experience the joy and reward of new beginnings in relationships. The difference is that this time around, my hope isn't in people. My hope is in the Lord, so no matter how others respond to what I do, I can rest knowing that when I do what *God* has asked me to do, I will be fulfilled. True satisfaction comes from following His will for our lives; it's just a bonus when we get to experience that fulfillment and satisfaction in our relationships with other people.

I have found that when I encourage someone, it makes me feel as good as they do. I've discovered how easy it is to make someone feel good by giving a gift or simply sending a "thinking of you" text or letter in the mail. When I sacrifice my own convenience to help someone else, even if they aren't appreciative, they might remember that they can count on me later on if they need help again. The same has been done for me and although I took it for granted before, I try my best to always express my gratitude now. Of course, it isn't always easy to love the way that Jesus does; but the hard stuff never made Him reluctant to do so, and it shouldn't stop us either.

This kind of openness and unity doesn't happen overnight, but as we trust the Lord and follow Him step by step, we come closer to togetherness like we've never known before. We just have to give time the opportunity to tell God's story through our lives and allow Him to unwind us, one step at a time.

13
Living Open

C.S. Lewis once said, "To love at all is to be vulnerable."[1] The beginning of vulnerability is not comfortable. In our culture and society, we have created this idea that if it makes you uncomfortable, you don't have to do it. And while this definitely holds some truth, we have started using it as an excuse, especially in regards to relationship. We no longer go the extra mile for people because we are too busy or too tired. We break up through text because having the conversation in person is too awkward. We bury our noses in social media so we don't have to engage in conversation with coworkers or strangers. Parents don't talk to their kids about sex (and we rarely hear about it in church for that matter) because it's "taboo." As a result, our children learn everything they know from the media and friends, and then the same happens for their kids after them because they were never taught to have the serious face-to-face talks that would later shape their standards and understanding of how life works.

We've begun to make sacrifices for the sake of convenience and it's a real shame.

The first time I really recognized this issue was in a worship service a while back. While I was singing, there were times I didn't know what to do with my hands. I know it sounds so silly because it doesn't really matter at all, but as a worship leader, it was something I was aware of. If you are comfortable, it's more likely that the people you are leading will engage with you and come along wherever you're going. Discomfort can sometimes be distracting.

I started to dive into that thought a little more and realized that we kind of do this a lot. I noticed that we tend to keep our hands full. It's more comfortable in conversation or sitting at work to be holding something or fidgeting with whatever is nearby. Even in worship, I sometimes find myself with my hands clasped in front on me because it feels weird to leave my arms down at my side. Maybe it's just me, but it seems like it's in our design to reach for something. We often cling to schedules, phones, social media, sports, work, whatever it may be, because when we have something to hold onto, we feel satisfied, accomplished, and secure. The downfall is that when our hands are full, it makes it much harder to receive.

We run into trouble when our hearts start to take on the same position of our hands. We internally cling to relationships, dreams, plans, and desires that leave us devastated if not fulfilled. It's true that hope deferred makes the heart sick.[2] Although it is far more comfortable to hold onto these things and fight to maintain control over them, it is only when we open our hearts to the Lord and surrender them to Him – however painful it may be – that He brings the true fulfillment our hearts are longing for. Releasing that which is most valuable to you is never an easy choice. It's scary and the deeper the hold, the more painful the ache left in the void it once filled; but our God is faithful to fill those places (if we let Him) and then return our things to us in proper order and perfect timing so to fulfill His plan just as much as our hearts. We just have to be brave enough to risk the discomfort in order to let go and receive the "more" God has for us.

I've heard it said that growth only happens outside the comfort zone. This is especially true when it comes to relationships. As you get acquainted with someone, the level of intimacy is based on the level of vulnerability. If you keep surface level conversations, you will have surface level relationship. The more you open up, the deeper the relationship and the greater the intimacy. It's like our relationship with the Lord: as we come to Him in boldness and honesty and surrender, the more He fills us up and the closer we become to Him as He transforms us into His likeness. There is an exchange of self for self that is most gratifying. In other words, this can sometimes mean that the greater the risk, the greater the reward.

The Lord showed me this idea once through a shovel. In this particular illustration, I was being referred to as the shovel. He was teaching me about relationships and how we often have to patiently endure and go deeper for the reward (like buried treasure). Not that we dig solely to get the reward, but we dig knowing that at some point our efforts will be worth everything we've invested in the process. If you can imagine someone digging a hole, there is bound to be some rocks or bugs or rusted old junk metal buried below the surface. The soil might be tough to break through in places, dry and cracked, or muddy at times; but if we gave up, we would never know what lies just a little further down. We would miss out on the potential treasures to be found.

As I was thinking this through, I realized that this kind of digging would require a lot of strength. If I were actually outside digging a hole (especially in the heat of Texas summer), I would quickly become exhausted and tempted to throw in the towel. It would hurt to drive my shovel deep into the ground and hit a rock, and I might even wake up sore the next day. It would be discouraging to give it my all and then find only more dirt after the dozens of shovelfuls I had already removed. And I don't even want to think about the frustration I would feel after a hard day's work if it began to rain and turn everything I had just worked for back to mush.

Almost bothered by the lesson, I thought to myself, "How could I possibly love people that way? I sure don't have that much determination or endurance. My strength would certainly fail within a few layers deep." And as I began to list the reasons why I can't, God tapped me on the shoulder and reminded me that He had only said that I was the shovel. *He* is the Gardener, the one who takes on the heavy load. I am only a vessel for His work, a clay jar He chooses (for reasons beyond me) to fill to overflowing so that His presence will permeate the earth like it is in heaven. He is always faithful to do His part. It's then up to me to be willing to open up enough for everything He has filled me with to spill out into the world around me.

It can be uncomfortable to begin opening your heart, especially if you've been hurt in relationships before, but it is the only way we truly get to enjoy the fulfillment found in God's perfect design for relationships. It takes time, but if we live with our hands and hearts open, they will never be empty.

The power of our stories is more than I think we understand. So often we shy away from sharing what God has done and is doing in our lives because we're afraid or convinced that no one will care. We can go on for years believing that we have nothing to offer God or the world, but the truth is that God is the One who authors and perfects our faith[3], and the stories He writes are never boring, insignificant, or useless. Everything He does and creates is intentional and filled to the brim with purpose, and that includes you and your life. I can't help but think He is on the edge of His seat waiting for you to see what He has in store as you turn the pages.

Telling your story doesn't necessarily mean that you have to spill your guts in every conversation. It can as simple as sharing the small things, the wonder that He reveals in the daily details. I have found that those kinds of conversations are so life-giving. It can be weird at first to open up about your story or listen to someone else's, but we can gradually work our way into God's original intent. He desires for us to be comfortable being open and honest with Him any time, and being made in His image, He desires the same for our relationships with other people. It is important to be patient. Give yourself and others lots of grace. Vulnerability can't be rushed, but when it is gently nurtured into fullness it is a wonderful gift that nothing can compare to.

In telling you my story, my hope was that you would find bits and pieces that relate to your own. I pray that you find comfort in the midst of your brokenness, purpose in the trials, and encouragement for your disappointments. There is hope for every story; no matter what chapter you're in right now. There is redemption and restoration for every broken heart because we serve a God who provides strength in our weakness and turns our pain into something beautiful.

As we become a Body that operates in honesty and openness, the key ingredient is love. I learned in my "Love Is" journey[4] that love creates a safe place for vulnerability. It is loving that leads us to be vulnerable; and it is in the vulnerability of the giving and receiving of love (to and from God and others) that we find our healing and freedom. So as we begin to open up and learn to love and be loved by Jesus, ever becoming more like Him, He unwinds us and draws us out of hiding and into relationship with kindness and compassion. There is so much grace for the becoming, so much safety in the risk of opening up before Him.

When we have found ourselves in Him, it gets easier to share our hearts with others. The closer we get to the Father, the more He reveals His heart to us, which in turn teaches us how to love Him, ourselves, and others the way we were created to. In this kind of love, vulnerability can thrive and pave the way for togetherness like our world has never known.

I encourage you to step into the fullness that God has for you. Be awakened to the fact that your life is significant and your story matters. So whatever your story is, remember that you have one. Dare to take the risk and experience the wonder of a life lived open.

"This is the message we heard from Jesus and now declare to you: God is light, and there is no darkness in Him at all. So we are lying if we say we have fellowship with God but go on living in spiritual darkness; we are not practicing the truth. But if we are living in the light, as God is in the light, then we have fellowship with each other, and the blood of Jesus, His Son, cleanses us from all sin." 1 John 1:5-7 (NLT)

Epilogue

Well, I wish I could sit here on the other side of these pages and tell you that it's been a breeze. I wish I could say that it's only been up and that once I learned all of these things, my life suddenly became easy and I never struggled in those areas I talked about again, but that's not how it works.

One of my teachers always used to say, "New levels, new devils." The more we grow and mature in the Lord, the bigger giants we face. It's like when Jesus told us that when we are faithful with a little, we would be given more.[1] As Christians, we are given the divine privilege of housing the greatest power of all: the very Spirit of Jesus Christ poured out to live inside of us, giving us full and complete access to the Father through Jesus at all times. However, the more we tap into the resources He has made available to us, the deeper we move into the battle.

As we continue to grow and He reveals more and more to us about Himself, His nature, and our enemy, He then trusts us to take on more responsibility. We are each responsible for the truth we have received, so when troubles and conflict come, we have a choice to either run and hide or stay and fight, taking advantage of the equipment He has armed us with (see Ephesians 6:10-18, 1 John 5:18, and Psalm 91:4 for just a few examples). He promises our protection and His promises *are* our protection. We just have to choose to stay close to Him and not turn our backs or blame Him when things get hard or don't make sense. He is on our side and fighting for us.[2]

A lot has happened since I left Christ for the Nations Institute in 2015 and I continue to grow in my church and in my personal relationship with the Lord. My body has healed from over six years of damage caused by eating disorders, I haven't sunken back into depression, I am happy and I now have the best relationships I have ever had. I have grown closer to Him and to other people, and as a result, more things have surfaced in my heart to be dealt with. However, God never gives us more than we can handle with His help. Even when it seems overwhelming, we can rest knowing He won't surface something until He sees that we are ready to deal with it. Sometimes it's very uncomfortable, but I have to remind myself that the pain of facing what's in my heart in order to get to freedom is much better than the continual ache of avoiding the hurt that has been stored up and harbored in my heart.

Since I have chosen to endure and embrace the process (which wasn't an immediate, willing response; rather, it was a gradual understanding of His heart that led to a trusting, "Okay, if this is what it will take.") I have been able to see the beauty of what He did with my obedience on the other side. Now that I know Him better, I welcome the hard stuff knowing that He uses even the most painful challenges as opportunities for more closeness as He refines us and invites us to partner with Him in bringing heaven to earth (even in the small things).

Several people have asked me about how I got closer to the Lord. I never really know how to answer because so much of our relationship has developed in the moments. In these past few years, I have come to understand how important it is to stick with Him, to be aware of His presence and what He is doing in my life and in the world around me. I had to learn the difference between being distant and distracted. The trick is communication.

For so long, I wouldn't ask God questions or take the time to really study the Bible because I was afraid I wouldn't hear His answer or I didn't really "have the time" to sit down and listen; but I have found two things to be true:

1. If you wait until you have time, you never will. You have to *make* the time.

People make time for the things they value. It took me a while to really grasp this concept. For some time, my morning devotions were more like part of a routine or habit than building a relationship with God. It became monotonous. It was tiring, dull, and even religious at times. I wasn't growing much because I hardly retained anything I was reading and there was no real substance to what I was doing because I viewed my time with God as part of a to-do list. Once I stopped doing it just to do it and instead began to set aside time in my day (or sometime during the week) to actually **listen**, things started changing. I started having my quiet time later in the day when I was more alert and could focus on what I was reading, or I would spend some time reading in the evening and journaling. The difference was that I started doing it because I *wanted* to. After a while I was starting my mornings with prayer and actually enjoying it, feeling like I was connecting with God rather than just doing my part so He would be happy. Which leads me to the second thing:

2. God loves and welcomes our honesty.

I don't think God is bothered at all when we are honest with Him. In fact, I think it makes Him happy when we feel comfortable enough in His presence to spill our guts. When we are open and vulnerable with God, He takes what we spill out and fills the void left over with Himself. It's a pretty wonderful exchange.

When beginning this process of opening up, most people say they don't know where to start. I remember feeling the same way when I was first trying to clear out all of the "stuff" so I could be closer to God. It can be a little awkward, like starting a new friendship (because it kind of is). For me, my internal world (my thought life) became so cluttered that His living accommodations in my heart were hardly viable for the life He was trying to offer me. I had shoved so many things down that it clogged up our passageway of communication. I picture it kind of like a tunnel or a cylinder (like a vase, for the sake of all my garden examples). I was so filled up with worries, fears, doubts, and suppressed pain that nothing and no one could easily pass through and get to my heart anymore, the place God was trying to reach so He could heal and restore. He couldn't come plow up the soil of my heart, uproot the weeds, and plant new life until we got past all the rocks at the surface. Thankfully, He isn't in a hurry. He takes the time to carefully take us over and through every obstacle.

When I realized how desperately I needed His help in order to undo all of it, I called out for Him and He answered me. One by one, the Holy Spirit began unloading everything I had packed away and addressing each bit of the blockage until the passageway was clear again and the weight was fully lifted.

Think of it like you've been away and you're coming back to catch up with a good friend you haven't connected with in a while. You would start where you left off, filling them in on every detail since you last met, whether that would take a few minutes or a few hours. Then you could carry on with life as usual, taking every step from there together. It's like that with Jesus. He loves to be close to us and He loves hearing everything we have to say. We just have to remember that a relationship with Him is the same as any other relationship, and we have to give Him room and time to speak to us as well.

As healthy dialogue develops in relationship, so does intimacy. The more we communicate with God and start to understand the truth of who He is and who we are in Him, the more comfortable we become being vulnerable in His presence. As a result, it becomes easier to open up and build relationships with others.

I'm not saying that once you get to a certain point it isn't hard anymore; I'm saying it's a daily choice. It just gets easier to choose the closer you get to Jesus, even when it's hard, because you start seeing things the way He does. That's what He's been teaching me in the meantime.

I'm still a work in progress. All of us will always be a work in progress, but that's all He wants us to be. He just wants us to be His.

My prayer is that we will all be able to embrace every step of the way, every part of the process, and enjoy His presence in the midst of all of it.

"I pray that God, the source of hope, will fill you completely with joy and peace because you trust in him. Then you will overflow with confident hope through the power of the Holy Spirit." Romans 15:13 (NLT)

Acknowledgements

To you, the reader, thank you for lending an ear to my story and for letting me share my heart with you. I wish that I could sit down and talk with you and listen to your story as well. Maybe someday we will find ourselves in a coffee shop somewhere doing exactly that. I hope that's the case, but even if not, know that I have prayed for you on your journey through these pages. I don't take lightly the fact that you chose this book out of the many others that would have been an excellent read. Thank you for sticking it out with me. You made the whole process worth it.

To Ryan (and Jess and Mom), for editing the crap out of this book even though you didn't have to. You did such a good job and I so appreciate your patience and brutal honesty. It's made me a better writer. Thank you for all of your hard work.

To Mom and Dad, for loving me before I ever did anything to deserve it. Thank you for supporting and believing in me even when I was lazy and stubborn. Thank you for being there the whole time. I know I wouldn't be here without you.

To Miss Sandra, for loving me through my pain with more honesty and wisdom than anyone else has ever taken the time to spend on me. Thank you for sharing your heart and story with me. Knowing you has changed my life.

To my church family, for showing me what it's like to feel at home in the Body. You have loved me so well and words can't adequately describe my appreciation for every single one of you.

To Elise, Puckett, and Martin, for always taking the time to answer my questions and talk through life in all its adventures and misadventures. Your friendships have made me so much stronger because you have loved me in my weaknesses and encouraged me through the valleys. Thank you for being there every step of the way.

To every friend who has encouraged me and prayed for me during this process, thank you for caring. Thank you for listening and letting me run ideas by you. Thank you for laughing with me and crying with me and believing in me.

To Melody, who has loved me and supported me from the very beginning. I will never be able to thank you enough for all the opportunities you have given me to grow and follow my dreams. Thank you for never letting me give up or settle.

To Smoothie King (Rick, Debbie, Ricky, and all of my coworkers), for being so good to me and allowing me to write when it wasn't busy at work.

To Chick-Fil-A and White Rhino, for fueling the majority of my writing sessions. Bless you.

And most importantly, thank you to God who has been entirely faithful, even in my unfaithfulness and irresponsibility along the way. Thank you for giving me the words every single time I sat down to write. Thank you for giving me the strength to keep going when I felt overwhelmed and unqualified, the courage to overcome lies and longing for the approval of others, and the fear of literally becoming an open book. I have so much peace and satisfaction turning the pages of this book and looking at everything we've done together. You're my favorite person to be loved by. Thank you for graciously giving me this opportunity. It has been a spectacular, wonder-filled adventure and I look forward to the chapters ahead.

Endnotes

Introduction
1. Genesis 50:20, when Joseph is talking to his brothers about how God took everything he went through and turned it around for Joseph's good and His glory.
2. Sheets, Dutch. "Full Circle ("Do It Again")." Christ for the Nations Institute, Dallas. 2014.

Chapter 2
1. Lucado, Max, and Terri A. Gibbs. *Grace for the Moment: Inspirational Thoughts for Each Day of the Year*. Nashville, TN: J. Countryman, 2000. Print.
2. I base this idea off of 2 Corinthians 12:9-10 and Ephesians 3:20.
3. I talk more about this in my book, Love Is.

Chapter 4
1. Eldredge, John, and Stasi Eldredge. *Captivating: Unveiling the Mystery of a Woman's Soul*. Nashville: Nelson, 2005. Print.
2. Shirer, Priscilla Evans. *The Armor of God*. Nashville, TN: Lifeway, 2015. Print.

Chapter 5
1. If you struggle with depression, I encourage you to tell someone that you trust or a counselor. I understand that it can be very painful to open up because a lot of people don't know what this battle is like, but when you don't open up, you stay a victim. Don't be

ashamed of this struggle, because your vulnerability will pave the way for freedom.

Chapter 7
1. In John 15 we find greater clarity about this concept of abiding.

Chapter 8
1. Hill, Susan D. *Closer than Your Skin: Unwrapping the Mystery of Intimacy with God.* Colorado Springs, CO: Waterbrook, 2008. Print.
2. Kruger, C. Baxter. *Across All Worlds: Jesus inside Our Darkness: An Essay on Reconciliation in Honor of Professor James B. Torrance.* Vancouver, B.C.: Regent College, 2007. Print.

Chapter 10
1. This journey in my life of discovering the Father's heart through the study and practice of His love turned into a book I called "Love Is." I made my journals into a format where you can go through the same journey for yourself.
2. I do **not** recommend doing this without consulting a doctor first, as it is very dangerous and the transition should be handled with care (even if you feel direct instruction from the Lord). Just let your doctor know so that you can monitor how your body responds.

Chapter 11
1. Isaiah 53:5

2. John 4:43-54

Chapter 12
1. *Merriam-Webster*. Merriam-Webster, n.d.
   Web. 27 July 2015.
2. Psalm 18:2

Chapter 13
1. Lewis, C. S. *The Four Loves*. New York:
   Harcourt, Brace, 1960. Print.
2. Proverbs 13:12
3. Hebrews 12:2
4. See chapter 10 endnotes.

Epilogue
1. Luke 16:10
2. Exodus 14:14